MW00769467

Mountain Biking
Flagstaff
and Sedona

BRUCE GRUBBS

FALCON® Helena, Montana

A FALCON GUIDE®

Falcon® Publishing is continually expanding its list of recreational guidebooks. All books include detailed descriptions, accurate maps, and all information necessary for enjoyable trips. You can order extra copies of this book and get information and prices for other Falcon® books by writing Falcon, P.O. Box 1718, Helena, MT 59624 or calling toll free 1-800-582-2665. Also, please ask for a free copy of our current catalog. Visit our website at www.FalconOutdoors.com or contact us by e-mail at falcon@falconguide.com.

© 1999 Falcon® Publishing, Inc., Helena, Montana.
Printed in Canada.

1 2 3 4 5 6 7 8 9 0 TP 04 03 02 01 00 99

Falcon and FalconGuide are registered trademarks of Falcon® Publishing, Inc.

Cataloging-in-Publication Data

Grubbs, Bruce (Bruce O.)
    Mountain biking Flagstaff and Sedona / Bruce Grubbs.
        p.   cm.—(A FalconGuide)
    Includes index.
    ISBN 1-56044-801-6 (pbk.)
    1. All terrain cycling—Arizona—Flagstaff—Guidebooks. 2. All terrain cycling—Arizona—Sedona—Guidebooks. I. Title.
    II. Series: Falcon guide.
    GV1045.5.A62F534 1999
    796.6'3'0979133—dc21   98-50418
                                                CIP

CAUTION

Outdoor recreational activities are by their very nature potentially hazardous. All participants in such activities must assume responsibility for their own actions and safety. The information contained in this guidebook cannot replace sound judgment and good decision-making skills, which help reduce risk exposure, nor does the scope of this book allow for disclosure of all the potential hazards and risks involved in such activities.

    Learn as much as possible about the outdoor recreational activities in which you participate, prepare for the unexpected, and be cautious. The reward will be a safer and more enjoyable experience.

♻ Text pages printed on recycled paper.

Contents

Sedona

Acknowledgments

I'd like to thank the following people for their help with this book. For reviewing the manuscript and providing many helpful suggestions, John Eavis, Kaibab National Forest, and Brian Potualski, Lori Denton, and Bill Stafford, Coconino National Forest. Thanks to Jean Rukkila for her usual excellent job of proofreading from an outdoor perspective. Thanks to my riding friends for putting up with trail mapping and photography, especially Kirk Litman and Patrick Malotki. Thanks to Cosmic Cycles in Flagstaff for maintaining my bike, to Single Track Bikes for getting hard to find parts for my old bike, and to Absolute Bikes for bike rack advice. Thanks to Sedona Bike and Bean and Mountain Bike Heaven in Sedona, for trail advice. We all owe thanks to the individuals and groups who build and maintain the trails. Thanks to my editors at Falcon Publishing, Randall Green and John Burbidge, who helped turn my manuscript into a finished book. And finally, heartfelt thanks to Duart Martin for encouraging this project at every turn.

MAP LEGEND

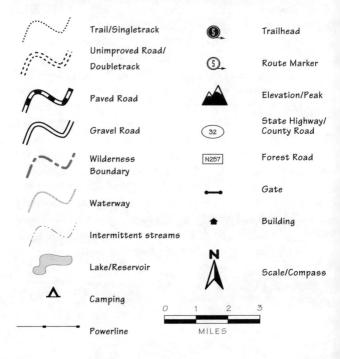

Trail/Singletrack		Trailhead	
Unimproved Road/Doubletrack		Route Marker	
Paved Road		Elevation/Peak	
Gravel Road		State Highway/County Road	32
Wilderness Boundary		Forest Road	N257
Waterway		Gate	
Intermittent streams		Building	
Lake/Reservoir			
Camping		Scale/Compass	N
Powerline			

0   1   2   3

MILES

• Flagstaff-Sedona Area

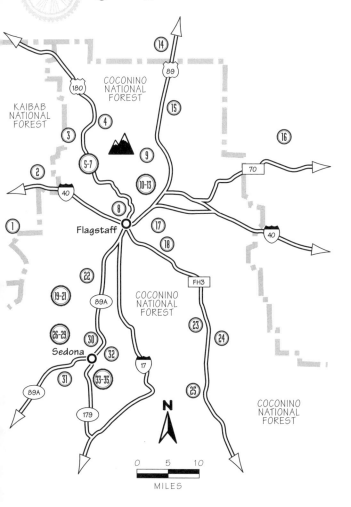

Get Ready to CRANK!

Where to ride? It's a quandary that faces every mountain biker, beginner or expert, local or tourist.

If you're new to the area, where do you start? If you're a long-time local, how do you avoid the rut of riding the same old trails week after week? And how do you find new terrain that's challenging but not overwhelming? Or an easier ride for when your not-so-serious buddies come along?

Welcome to *Mountain Biking Flagstaff and Sedona*. Here are 35 rides ranging from easy road routes to smooth singletrack to bravado-busting boulder fields. The rides are described in plain language, with accurate distances and ratings for aerobic level and technical difficulty. Each entry offers a wealth of detailed information that's easy to read and use, from an armchair or on the trail.

My aim is threefold: to help you choose a ride that's appropriate for your fitness and skill level; to make it easy to find the trailhead; and to help you complete the ride safely, without getting lost. Take care of those basics and fun is bound to break loose.

The Flagstaff and Sedona Areas: What to Expect

The rides in the Flagstaff-Sedona area cover a wide variety of terrain—from red rock desert canyons to forested plateaus to alpine mountains. That means two things: the trails are often steep and rough, and the weather can be unpredictable, and, at times, severe.

Arizona's terrain requires preparedness. Get in good shape before you attempt these rides, and know your limits. Clean and maintain your bike frequently. Before each ride, check tires, rims, brakes, handlebars, seat, shifters, derailleurs, and chain to make sure they survived the last ride and are functioning properly.

A helmet is essential for safe mountain biking; it can save your life and prevent serious injuries. Cycling gloves are another essential piece of safety equipment that can save hands from cuts and bruises from falls, encroaching branches, and rocks. They also improve your grip and comfort on the handlebars.

Always pack at least one (filled) water bottle. Rides in the Sedona area are hot in the summer and you'll want more water. A gallon is not too much on long, hot rides. A snack such as fruit or sports energy bars can keep those mighty thighs cranking for hours and prevent dreaded "bonk"—the sudden loss of energy when your body runs out of fuel. Dress for the weather and pack a wind- and waterproof jacket just in case. Many of the rides are above 7,000 feet, and at these altitudes the Arizona summer sun packs a wallop, even when the air is cool. Don't forget sunglasses, sunscreen, and lip balm. Insects can be a problem for a short period in the spring. In wet years, you may want to carry insect repellent.

It's wise to carry a small tool kit with appropriate tools for your bike, a spare tube, and a patch kit. A tire pump is a must. I also fill my tubes with leak repair goo, because of the thorns and spines on the desert rides. Some cacti grow at elevations as high as 8,000 feet; a ride through prickly pear will quickly use up all the patches you have!

This book is designed to be easily carried in a pocket or bike bag, and the maps and ride descriptions will help anyone unfamiliar with the trails. U.S. Geological Survey topographic maps can provide a more detailed view of the terrain, but ride routes may not be shown. The correct topo maps are listed for each ride. The majority of the rides are in the Coconino and Kaibab National Forests; USDA Forest Service maps are useful for finding the approach roads and some of the rides.

Finally—I'll say it again—always wear a helmet.

The **weather** in northern Arizona's high plateau country spans the range of North American extremes. On the San Francisco Peaks, snow can fall any month of the year. Summer highs routinely top 100 degrees F in the lower country. In general, higher elevations are cooler (by as much as 6 degrees F for every 1,000 feet) and windier. If you drive to a trailhead, play it safe and take a variety of clothes in the car to match the weather you're likely to encounter.

That said, we ride here year-round. Most of the trails near Flagstaff are rideable from May through November. In dry years, some trails can be ridden all winter. The best season around Sedona is September through May, though summer riding is pleasant early in the morning. (Bear in mind that hunting seasons may occur during the good fall riding weather. Check with the Arizona Game and Fish Department for current hunting seasons. See Appendix A. If you choose to ride during hunting season, a blaze orange vest is a sensible precaution.)

Afternoon thunderstorms are common during July, August, and September. These storms often appear suddenly and can be severe, with hail, high wind, and lightning. If caught in a thunderstorm, get off the high ridges and take shelter in a low-lying area or in a vehicle. Do not remain under lone trees. During thunderstorm season, the mornings generally dawn sweet and clear, the air refreshed by yesterday's showers. It's a good idea to complete your day's riding by noon.

The high plateau and the Mogollon Rim attract more rain and snow than does the Sedona-Verde Valley area. The low country does get some snow in the winter, but it usually melts on the first clear day. The rides in this book vary from 4,000 feet to over 10,000 feet in elevation, which means you really can ride dirt all year.

Please stay off wet, muddy trails—the soil damage and erosion that even one rider can cause is great.

IMBA Rules of the Trail

If every mountain biker always yielded the right-of-way, stayed on the trail, avoided wet or muddy trails, never cut switchbacks, always rode in control, showed respect for other trail users, and carried out every last scrap (candy wrappers and bike-part debris included) of what was carried in—in short, if we all *did the right thing*—we wouldn't need a list of rules governing our behavior.

Fact is, most mountain bikers are conscientious and are trying to do the right thing. No one becomes good at something as demanding and painful as grunting up mountainsides by cheating.

Most of us don't need rules.

But we do need knowledge of what exactly is the right thing to do.

Here are some guidelines, reprinted by permission from the International Mountain Bicycling Association. The basic idea is to prevent or minimize damage to land, water, plants, and wildlife, and to avoid conflicts with other backcountry visitors and trail users. Ride with respect.

Thousands of miles of dirt trails have been closed to mountain bicyclists. The irresponsible riding habits of a few riders have been a factor. Do your part to maintain trail access by observing the following rules of the trail, formulated by the International Mountain Bicycling Association (IMBA). IMBA's mission is to promote environmentally sound and socially responsible mountain biking.

1. Ride on open trails only. Respect trail and road closures (ask if not sure), avoid possible trespass on private land, obtain permits and authorization as may be required. Federal wilderness areas are closed to bicycles and all other mechanized and motorized equipment. The way you ride will influence trail management decisions and policies.

2. Leave no trace. Be sensitive to the dirt beneath you. Even on open (legal) trails, you should not ride under conditions where you will leave evidence of your passing, such as on certain soils after a rain. Recognize different types of soils and trail construction; practice low-impact cycling. This also means staying on existing trails and not creating new ones. Be sure to pack out at least as much as you pack in. Some of the rides feature optional side hikes into wilderness areas. Be a low impact hiker also.

3. Control your bicycle! Inattention for even a second can cause problems. Obey all bicycle speed regulations and recommendations.

4. Always yield trail. Make known your approach well in advance. A friendly greeting (or bell) is considerate and works well; don't startle others. Show your respect when passing by slowing to a walking pace or stopping. Anticipate other trail users at corners and blind spots.

5. Never spook animals. All animals are startled by an unannounced approach, a sudden movement, or a loud noise. This can be dangerous for you, others, and the animals. Give animals extra room and time to adjust to you. When passing horses use special care and follow directions from the horseback riders (dismount and ask if uncertain). Chasing cattle and disturbing wildlife is a serious offense. Leave gates as you found them, or as marked.

6. Plan ahead. Know your equipment, your ability, and the area in which you are riding—and prepare accordingly. Be self-sufficient at all times, keep your equipment in good repair, and carry necessary supplies for changes in weather or other conditions. A well-executed trip is a satisfaction to you and not a burden or offense to others. Always wear a helmet.

Keep trails open by setting a good example of environmentally sound and socially responsible off-road cycling.

How to use this Guide

Mountain Biking Flagstaff and Sedona describes 35 mountain bike rides in their entirety.

Many of the featured rides are loops, beginning and ending at the same point but coming and going on different trails. Loops are by far the most popular type of ride, and we're lucky to have so many in the area.

Be forewarned: the difficulty of a loop may change dramatically depending on which direction you ride around the loop. If you are unfamiliar with the rides in this book, try them first as described here. The directions follow the path of least resistance and most fun (which does not necessarily mean easy). After you've been over the terrain, you can determine whether a given loop would be fun—or even feasible—in the reverse direction.

Portions of some rides follow gravel or even paved roads, and there's one ride that's all road. Purists may wince at road rides in a book about mountain biking, but this one is special. Each ride description follows the same format:

Name: For the most part, I relied on official names of trails, roads, and natural features as shown on USDA Forest Service and U.S. Geological Survey maps. In some cases deference was given to long-term local custom.

Location: Distance and direction from Flagstaff or Sedona, and the general whereabouts of the ride.

Distance: The length of the ride in miles, given as a loop, one way, or out-and-back.

Time: A conservative estimate of how long it takes to complete the ride, for example, 1 to 2 hours. *The time listed is the actual riding time and does not include rest stops.* Strong, skilled riders may be able to do a given ride in less than the estimated time, while other riders may take considerably longer. Also bear in mind that severe weather, changes in trail conditions, or mechanical problems may prolong a ride.

Tread: The type of road or trail: paved road, maintained dirt road, doubletrack road, wide singletrack, or singletrack.

Aerobic level: The level of physical effort required to complete the ride: easy, moderate, or strenuous.

Easy: Flat or gently rolling terrain, with no steep or prolonged climbs.

Moderate: Some hills; the climbs may be short and fairly steep, or long and gradual. There may be short hills that less fit riders will want to walk.

Strenuous: Frequent or prolonged climbs steep enough to require riding in the lowest gear; requires a high level of aerobic fitness, power, and endurance (typically acquired through many hours of riding and proper training). Less fit riders may need to walk.

Many rides are mostly easy and moderate but may have short strenuous sections. Other rides are mostly strenuous and should be attempted only after a complete medical checkup and implant of a second heart, preferably a big one. Also be aware that thrashing through a highly technical section can be exhausting even on the flats. Good riding skills and a relaxed stance on the bike save energy.

Finally, any ride can be strenuous if you ride it hard and fast. Conversely, the pain of a lung-burning climb grows easier to tolerate as your fitness level improves. Learn to pace yourself and remember to schedule easy rides and rest days into your calendar.

Technical difficulty: The level of bike handling skills needed to complete the ride upright and in one piece. Technical difficulty is rated on a scale of 1 to 5, with 1 being the easiest and 5 the hardest.

Level 1: Smooth tread; road or doubletrack; no obstacles, ruts, or steeps. Requires basic bike-handling skills.

Level 2: Mostly smooth tread; wide, well-groomed singletrack or road/doubletrack with minor ruts or loose gravel or sand.

Level 3: Irregular tread with some rough sections; slickrock, single- or doubletrack with obvious route choices; some steep sections; occasional obstacles may include small rocks, roots, water bars, ruts, loose gravel or sand, and sharp turns or broad, open switchbacks.

Level 4: Rough tread with few smooth places; singletrack or rough doubletrack with limited route choices; steep sections, some with obstacles; obstacles are numerous and varied, including rocks, roots, branches, ruts, sidehills, narrow tread, loose gravel or sand, and switchbacks. Most slickrock falls in this level.

Level 5: Continuously broken, rocky, root-infested, or trenched tread; singletrack or extremely rough doubletrack with few route choices; frequent, sudden, and severe changes in gradient; some slopes so steep that wheels lift off ground; obstacles are nearly continuous and may include boulders, logs, water, large holes, deep ruts, ledges, piles of loose gravel, steep sidehills, encroaching trees, and tight switchbacks.

I've also added plus (+) and minus (-) symbols to cover gray areas between given levels of difficulty; a 4+ obstacle is harder than a 4, but easier than a 5-. A stretch of trail rated 5+ would be unrideable by all but the most skilled riders.

Again, most of the rides in this book cover varied terrain, with an ever-changing degree of technical difficulty. Some trails run smoothly with only occasional obstacles, and other trails are seemingly all obstacles. The path of least resistance, or line, is where you find it. In general, most obstacles are more challenging if you encounter them while climbing than while descending. On the other hand, in heavy surf (boulder fields, tangles of downfall, cliffs), fear plays a larger role when facing downhill.

Understand that different riders have different strengths and weaknesses. Some folks can scramble over logs and boulders without a grunt, but they crash head over heels on every switchback turn. Some fly off the steepest slopes and others freeze. Some riders climb like the wind and others just blow . . . and walk.

The key to overcoming "technical difficulties" is practice; keep trying. Follow a rider who makes it look easy, and don't hesitate to ask for constructive criticism. Try shifting your weight (good riders move a lot, front to back, side to side, and up and down) and experimenting with balance and momentum. Find a smooth patch of lawn and practice riding as slowly as possible, even balancing in a "track stand" (described in the Glossary). This will give you more confidence—and more time to recover or bail out—the next time the trail rears up and bites.

Hazards: A list of dangers that may be encountered on a ride, including traffic, weather, trail obstacles and conditions, risky stream crossings, obscure trails, and other perils. Remember: conditions may change at any time. Be alert for storms, fences, deadfall, missing trail signs, and mechanical failure. Fatigue, heat, cold, and/or dehydration may impair judgment. Always wear a helmet and other safety equipment. Ride in control at all times.

Highlights: Special features or qualities that make a ride worth doing (as if we needed an excuse!): scenery, fun singletrack, chances to see wildlife.

Land status: A list of managing agencies or landowners. Most of the rides in this book are in the Coconino National Forest. But many of the rides also cross portions of private, state, county, or municipal lands. Always leave gates as you found them, or as signed. And respect the land and property, regardless of who owns it. See Appendix A for a list of Forest Service addresses.

Maps: A list of available maps. The Coconino National Forest map at a scale of 1:126,720 affords a good overview of travel routes in the area. USGS topographic maps in the 7.5-minute series give a close-up look at terrain. The *Arizona Atlas* published by DeLorme Mapping at a scale of 1:250,000 gives a good topographic overview. Not all routes are shown on official maps.

Access: How to find the trailhead or the start of the ride. A number of rides can be pedaled right from the towns; for others it's best to drive to the trailhead.

The Ride: A mile-by-mile list of key points—landmarks, notable climbs and descents, stream crossings, obstacles, hazards, major turns, and junctions—along the ride. All distances were measured to the hundredth of a mile (they were rounded to the nearest tenth for the listing) with a carefully calibrated cyclometer. As a result, you will find a cyclometer to be very useful for following the descriptions. Trails were carefully mapped using the USGS 7.5-minute topographic maps as a reference. A GPS

(Global Positioning System) receiver was used to supplement more traditional methods of land navigation where landmarks were obscure. Terrain, riding technique, and even tire pressure can affect odometer readings, so treat all mileages as estimates.

Finally, one last reminder—the real world is changing all the time. The information presented here is as accurate and up-to-date as possible, but there are no guarantees out in the backcountry. You alone are responsible for your safety and for the choices you make on the trail.

If you do find an error or omission in this book, or a new and noteworthy change in a ride, I'd like to hear from you. Please write to Bruce Grubbs, c/o Falcon Publishing, P.O. Box 1718, Helena, MT 59624.

Elevation Graphs

An elevation profile accompanies each ride description. Here the ups and downs of the route are graphed on a grid of elevation (in feet above sea level) on the left and miles pedaled across the bottom. Route surface conditions (see map legend), and technical levels are shown on the graphs.

Note that these graphs are compressed (squeezed) to fit on the page. The actual slopes you will ride are not as steep as the lines drawn on the graphs (it just feels that way). Also, some extremely short dips and climbs are too small to show up on the graphs. All such abrupt changes in gradient are, however, mentioned in the mile-by-mile ride description.

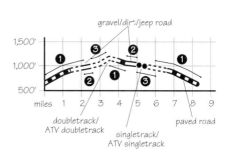

The Name Game

Mountain bikers often assign their own descriptive nicknames to trails.

These nicknames may help to distinguish or describe certain parts of the overall ride, but only for the group of people that know the nickname. All too often the nicknames are meaningless (or misleading) to cyclists who haven't spun their pedals on the weekly group ride.

For the sake of clarity, I stuck to the official (or at least most widely accepted) names for the trails and roads described in this book. When a route is commonly known by more than one name, the other names are mentioned. If you know them by some other name, or if you come up with nicknames that peg the personalities of these rides, by all means share them with your riding buddies.

Sycamore Rim

Location: 28 miles west of Flagstaff at the head of Sycamore Canyon.

Distance: 7.2 miles out and back.

Time: 2 hours.

Tread: 7.2 miles on singletrack.

Aerobic level: Easy.

Technical difficulty: 3.

Hazards: Occasional rocky stretches of trail.

Highlights: This singletrack skirts the rim of Sycamore Canyon at its headwaters and offers views of the rugged Sycamore Canyon Wilderness. The riding is mostly smooth, fast singletrack.

Land status: Kaibab National Forest.

Maps: USGS Garland Prairie, Davenport Hill; Kaibab National Forest (Tusayan, Williams, and Chalender Ranger Districts).

Access: From Flagstaff, drive 13.6 miles west on Interstate 40, then exit at Parks. Turn left onto Garland Prairie Road (Forest Road 141). Go 9.7 miles, then turn left on FR 131. Continue 0.6 mile, and park at Dow Spring Trailhead on the right.

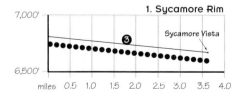

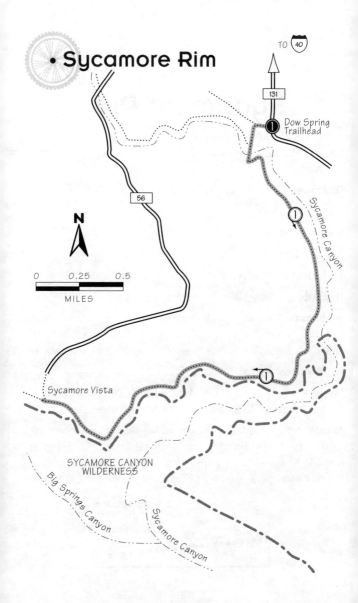

• Sycamore Rim

TO 40

131

Dow Spring
Trailhead

Sycamore Canyon

56

N

0   0.25   0.5

MILES

Sycamore Vista

SYCAMORE CANYON
WILDERNESS

Big Springs Canyon

Sycamore Canyon

The Ride

0.0   Pedal west out of the parking lot.

0.1   Hang a left at Overland Trail junction, and ride over an old railroad grade. Around the turn of the century, temporary rail lines were constructed to active logging areas. Afterward, the rails were removed, leaving the railroad grade and wooden ties.

0.2   Turn left on Sycamore Rim Trail. The tread is mostly smooth singletrack except for a few short rocky sections. Sycamore Canyon deepens as you ride its west rim.

3.6   A sign marks Sycamore Vista. You're looking south into the Sycamore Canyon Wilderness near the confluence of Big Spring Canyon and Sycamore Canyon. This is the turn-around point; the section of trail to the west enters Sycamore Wilderness, which is closed to bikes. Retrace your tracks to the trailhead.

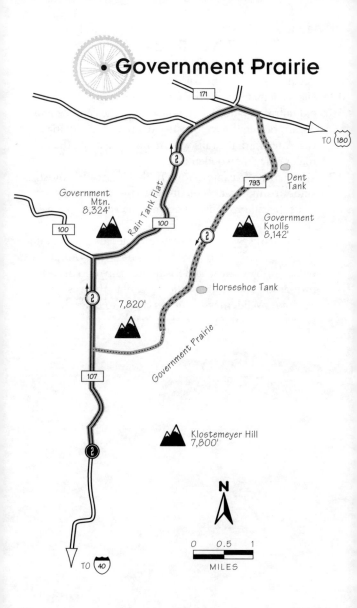

Government Prairie

171

TO (180)

2

793

Dent
Tank

Government
Mtn.
8,324'

100   100

Rain Tank Flat

2

Government
Knolls
8,142'

2

Horseshoe Tank

7,820'

Government Prairie

107

Klostemeyer Hill
7,800'

2

N

TO (40)

0   0.5   1
MILES

Government Prairie

Location: 21 miles west of Flagstaff.

Distance: 15.2-mile loop.

Time: 3 hours.

Tread: 9 miles on maintained dirt, 4.8 miles on doubletrack, 1.4 miles on singletrack.

Aerobic level: Easy.

Technical difficulty: 1 on maintained dirt, 2 on double- and singletrack.

Hazards: Large prairie dog holes along double- and single-track.

Highlights: Nearly level, easy cruise through extensive meadows and forest.

Land status: Kaibab National Forest, private.

Maps: USGS Parks, Moritz Ridge, Kendrick Peak, Wing Mountain; Kaibab National Forest (Tusayan, Williams, and Chalender Ranger Districts).

Access: From Flagstaff, drive about 17 miles west on Interstate 40, then take the Parks exit. Turn right (north), and after 0.1 mile turn right again at a T intersection. Follow this paved road 0.8 mile (the former route of historic U.S. Highway 66), past the end of pavement, then turn left onto Forest Road 107. Drive 3.2 miles on this maintained dirt road. The road emerges onto scenic Government Prairie as it enters a small subdivision. Park at the turn-around where the road narrows at the north end of the subdivision.

The Ride

0.0 Starting point at the turn-around. FR 107 is still maintained but becomes narrower. The hills visible across Government Prairie are all extinct volcanic cinder cones.

2.1 Ride straight on FR 107 (FR 793 branches right). The road soon enters ponderosa pine forest.

3.2 Pedal right (east) on FR 100, which is also maintained dirt.

5.3 Ride into Rain Tank Flat, a small park. The road begins to climb gradually.

7.2 Swing right on FR 171, a maintained dirt road.

7.7 Take another right on FR 793, a doubletrack that can be rocky in places. It's a gentle downhill roll through the shady forest.

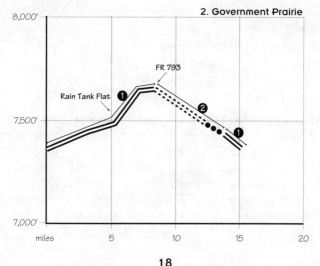

8.4 Pass through a wire gate at Dent Tank, cross a section of private land, and cruise onto the northern end of Government Prairie.

8.8 Unmarked junction; stay right along the northwest side of the meadow.

10.3 Another wire gate.

11.2 Multiple doubletracks go right at Horseshoe Tank; continue straight on FR 793.

12.3 Yet another wire gate; this time, go straight on a faint doubletrack, leaving FR 793. The next section of the ride follows old closed roads and cattle trails for 1.4 miles.

12.5 Turn left at a crossroads where there is a small cattle watering trough. The old road is closed to motorized travel and has been rehabilitated by the Forest Service, but you can follow a rocky cattle trail with little difficulty. Yes, cows like singletrack too! Watch for fresh droppings, though. Another hazard is occasional large prairie dog holes in the track. If you're lucky you may see one of the diggers keeping a wary lookout. More likely, you'll hear the warning whistle as the prairie dog ducks back in his den.

13.2 Another cattle trough marks a split in the cattle trails. Ride the one to the right, which skirts the base of the nearby cinder cone. The cow trail soon joins another old closed road and swings around the rocky south base of the hill.

13.9 Ride along the left side of a stock tank, then ride southwest to join FR 107. Turn left to ride back to the trailhead.

15.2 End of the ride at the parking area.

Kendrick Mountain

Location: About 20 miles northwest of Flagstaff at the base of Kendrick Mountain.

Distance: 24.2-mile loop.

Time: 4 hours.

Tread: 6.8 miles on doubletrack, 17.4 miles on maintained dirt road of various quality.

Aerobic level: Moderate.

Technical difficulty: 1 on maintained dirt, 2 on doubletrack.

Hazards: Deep ruts on sections of the doubletrack. The ride skirts the Kendrick Mountain Wilderness on roads; trails in the wilderness area are closed to bicycles.

Highlights: A long, scenic cruise around the fourth highest mountain in the state.

Land status: Kaibab National Forest, Coconino National Forest, private.

Maps: USGS Kendrick Peak, Wing Mountain, Moritz Ridge; Coconino National Forest; Kaibab National Forest (Tusayan, Williams, and Chalender Ranger Districts).

Access: From Flagstaff, drive north on U.S. Highway 180, passing the turnoff to the Arizona Snowbowl Ski Area about 7 miles from town. Continue 10 more miles, then turn left on Forest Road 193, a maintained dirt road signed for Kendrick Peak. Go 1.8 miles and park where a doubletrack, FR 9020A, joins the main road from the right. Kendrick Peak is visible to the northwest.

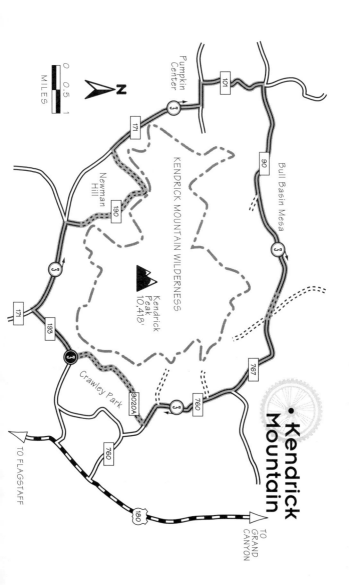

Kendrick Mountain

KENDRICK MOUNTAIN WILDERNESS

Kendrick Peak
10,418'

Pumpkin Center

Newman Hill

Bull Basin Mesa

Crawley Park

TO FLAGSTAFF

TO GRAND CANYON

N

MILES
0   0.5   1

101
90
171
190
171
193
767
760
9020A
760
180

The Ride

0.0   Start off by continuing west on FR 193, which becomes a gradual downhill roll.

1.5   Pedal right on FR 171, another maintained dirt road.

3.6   Go right again on FR 190, signed for Kendrick Trail.

4.1   Pass the Kendrick Trailhead, which is on the right. (The trail enters Kendrick Wilderness, which is closed to bicycles.) Continue on the road, which becomes doubletrack and starts to climb steadily through pine and aspen forest.

4.9   Ride through the saddle between Kendrick Peak and Newman Hill, the high point of the ride, and start down.

6.2   The descent moderates.

7.1   Go right on FR 171, which is maintained dirt. You're now descending gradually along the southwest slopes of the mountain.

9.0   Ride past Pumpkin Center, an old settlement.

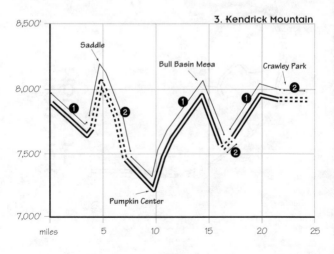

3. Kendrick Mountain

9.4   Hang a sharp left to stay on FR 171, the main road.

9.8   This is the lowest point along the ride. Pedal right onto FR 101, a poorly maintained road. It skirts the west edge of the Pumpkin Center meadow, then starts to climb steadily.

10.8 The grade moderates, but the road continues to climb onto Bull Basin Mesa.

11.6 Swing right onto FR 90, a maintained dirt road, which continues to climb.

14.3 Turn left to stay on FR 90, which soon starts to descend to the east. The aspen and fir-covered north slopes of Kendrick Peak are sometimes visible to the south.

16.2 The descent moderates as the road becomes rough doubletrack.

16.7 The road becomes FR 760A and starts to climb as you ride into the Coconino National Forest.

17.4 Continue straight onto FR 767, a smooth maintained dirt road that climbs steadily southeast through pine forest.

19.3 Turn right on FR 191C, also a maintained dirt road.

19.9 Turn left on FR 760, which is a maintained dirt road.

21.6 In a meadow, turn right onto FR 9020A, a doubletrack that leads past a stock tank and then along the west side of Crawley Park.

22.8 Wire gate.

23.3 Bear left (south) at an unsigned junction.

24.2 FR 9020A ends at FR 193 and your vehicle.

Saddle Mountain

Location: 20 miles northwest of Flagstaff, on the northwest side of the San Francisco Peaks.

Distance: 14.8 miles out and back.

Time: 3 hours.

Tread: 6 miles on doubletrack, 8.8 miles on maintained dirt road.

Aerobic level: Moderate.

Technical difficulty: 1 on maintained dirt, 2 on doubletrack.

Hazards: Washouts and patches of loose cinders on Saddle Mountain Road.

Highlights: A very scenic ride through alpine meadows to the top of an old volcano; 50-mile views.

Land status: Coconino National Forest.

Maps: USGS Kendrick Peak, White Horse Hills; Coconino National Forest.

Access: From Flagstaff, drive north on U.S. Highway 180, passing the turnoff to the Arizona Snowbowl Ski Area about 7 miles from town. Continue another 13.6 miles into Kendrick Park, and park on the right at the junction with Forest Road 514.

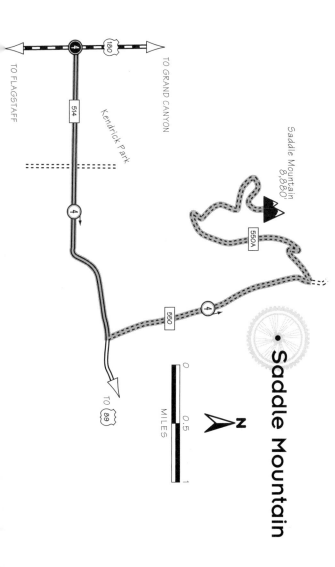

TO FLAGSTAFF

TO GRAND CANYON

180

514

Kendrick Park

4

Saddle Mountain
8,880'

550A

550

4

TO 89

0   0.5   1
MILES

N

Saddle Mountain

The Ride

0.0 Junction of US 180 and FR 514. Ride east on FR 514, a maintained dirt road, across the open expanse of Kendrick Park. The towering San Francisco Peaks dominate the skyline to the southeast, and Saddle Mountain is visible to the northeast.

1.7 Start a gentle downhill coast as the road enters the pine forest.

2.6 Hang a sharp left on FR 550, and pedal north up a gentle hill. The road passes through a series of meadows, then climbs to a junction at the head of the valley.

4.4 Ride left on FR 550A, Saddle Mountain Road. Follow the doubletrack as it climbs gradually west, headed toward the summit of Saddle Mountain.

4.9 A single switchback leads to an open view on the ridgetop. The cliffs of the Grand Canyon are usually visible 50 miles to the north. To the south, the valley you just rode through spreads out below. The peculiar pattern of meadows, scraggly pines, and patches of trees of uniform height are all evidence of past forest fires.

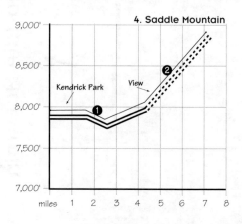

4. Saddle Mountain

The scraggly trees are survivors; the uniform patches are trees that were planted after the fire. A large fire in 1996 burned the White Horse Hills, visible to the south at the foot of the San Francisco Peaks. Back on the ride, you'll find that the road continues at a steady but moderate grade all the way to the summit. It wraps around the mountain, giving you views in all directions as you climb.

7.4 Saddle Mountain summit. A Forest Service radio site marks the summit. The road was originally built to provide access to a fire lookout tower, since removed. Turn around and retrace your tracks to US 180. On the descent, watch out for sudden loose patches of cinders and occasional deep ruts caused by heavy summer rains.

Lava River Cave

Location: 10 miles northwest of Flagstaff, west of the San Francisco Peaks.

Distance: 18.2 miles out and back.

Time: 2 to 3 hours.

Tread: 0.6 mile on doubletrack, 17.6 miles on maintained dirt road.

Aerobic level: Easy.

Technical difficulty: 1 on maintained dirt road, 2 on doubletrack.

Hazards: Traffic on dirt roads.

Highlights: This is a relaxing, scenic cruise through pine forest and meadows with little elevation change. Your destination is a lava tube cave. This type of cavern forms when molten lava, flowing through an underground passage, subsides and leaves a long, tube-like cave.

Land status: Coconino National Forest.

Maps: USGS Wing Mountain; Coconino National Forest.

Access: From Flagstaff, drive north on U.S. Highway 180, passing the turnoff to the Arizona Snowbowl Ski Area about 7 miles from town. Continue another 3 miles, then turn left on Forest Road 222B. This junction is signed for parking, and is just past the Hart Prairie Road. Park along the side of the dirt road.

The Ride

0.0 Pedal west along the maintained dirt road, FR 222B.
0.6 Signed trailhead and parking for the Wing Mountain

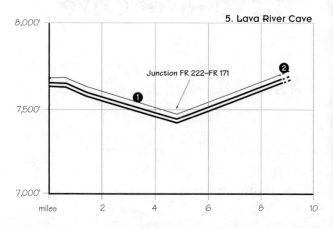

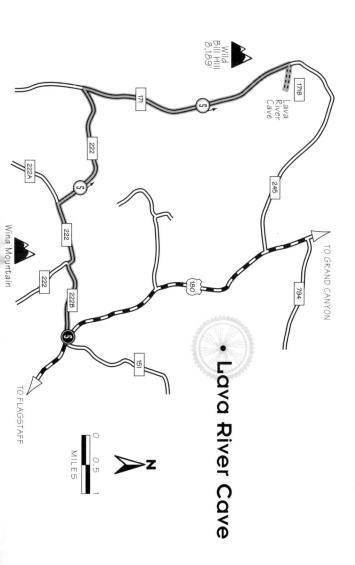

Lava River Cave

Wild
Bill Hill
8,189

171
171B
Lava
River
Cave
245

Wina Mountain

222
222A
222
222
222B
180
794

151

TO GRAND CANYON

TO FLAGSTAFF

N

0   0.5   1
MILES

Cross Country Ski Area. Turn right, remaining on FR 222B. The wider road goes left but dead ends in a cinder pit.

0.8   Bear left at a stock tank, remaining on FR 222B.

1.3   Turn right at the T intersection, going west on FR 222.

2.3   Bear right at the junction with FR 222A; stay on FR 222.

4.8   Turn sharply right on FR 171.

6.7   The road enters a long, narrow meadow.

8.8   Turn right on FR 171B, a doubletrack that can be muddy after rain or snow melt.

9.1   Signed parking for Lava River Cave. The cave entrance is a pit formed when part of the cave roof collapsed. Scramble down over jumbled lava blocks to reach the floor of the cave. If you explore further, bring at least three sources of light, and use a lock to secure your bike. The cave is a single passage about 0.75 mile in length. After spelunking, ride the same route back to your car.

Hart Prairie

Location: About 13 miles northwest of Flagstaff, on the west slopes of the San Francisco Peaks.

Distance: 6.2-mile loop.

Time: 1 hour.

Tread: 2 miles on doubletrack, 2 miles on maintained dirt, 2.2 miles on paved road.

Aerobic level: Moderate.

Technical difficulty: 2+ on doubletrack, 1 on maintained dirt and pavement.

Hazards: Heavy traffic on U.S. Highway 180 during summer.

Highlights: This is an easy ride through a delightful mix of ponderosa pine and quaking aspen forest and across alpine meadows.

Land status: Coconino National Forest.

Maps: USGS Wing Mountain, Humphreys Peak; Coconino National Forest.

Access: From Flagstaff, drive north on US 180, passing the turnoff to the Arizona Snowbowl Ski Area about 7 miles from town. Continue another 5.8 miles, then park at an unsigned turnoff on the right (Forest Road 9001L). This turnoff is on the outside of a left curve just after the highway enters the first aspen stands.

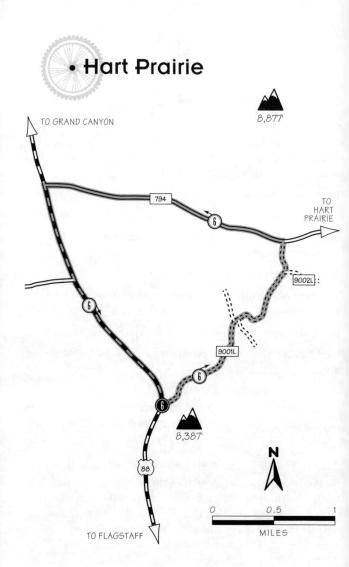

• Hart Prairie

TO GRAND CANYON

8,877'

794

6

TO HART PRAIRIE

9002L

9001L

6

6

8,387'

88

TO FLAGSTAFF

N

0   0.5   1

MILES

32

The Ride

0.0 Ride through the gate directly away from the highway on FR 9001L. Numerous side roads branch off in the next 2 miles; stay on the main road, which climbs steadily to the northeast.

1.1 Pedal straight ahead at a crossroads in a narrow meadow. The correct road goes east, uphill, and back into the aspens.

1.7 Go left at the junction with FR 9002L. The alpine meadow you're crossing is part of Hart Prairie, an extensive alpine meadow on the west side of the San Francisco Peaks.

2.0 Junction with FR 794. (If you want to do a longer ride and see more of Hart Prairie, turn right on FR 794, which becomes doubletrack, and ride about 1 mile to FR 151. Then turn right—the next mile of this road traverses Hart Prairie and offers fine views. The only catch is that it's a busy road during the summer.) To complete the loop from mile 2.0, pedal left onto FR 794, a maintained dirt road, and cruise down the gentle hill to US 180.

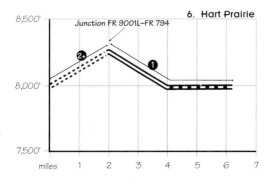

4.0 Turn left (south) on US 180. This highway is very busy with traffic heading to the Grand Canyon during the summer. Fortunately it's a fast, big ring crank back to the car.

6.2 End of the loop.

Wing Mountain

Location: About 9 miles northwest of Flagstaff, southwest of the San Francisco Peaks.

Distance: 10.2-mile loop.

Time: 1.5 hours.

Tread: 10.2 miles on maintained dirt road.

Aerobic level: Easy.

Technical difficulty: 1+.

Hazards: Light vehicle traffic on roads.

Highlights: An easy loop around an old volcano featuring great views of the high peaks.

Land status: Coconino National Forest.

Maps: USGS Wing Mountain, Humphreys Peak; Coconino National Forest.

Access: From the junction of Route 66 and U.S. Highway 180 in Flagstaff, drive north on US 180 about 7 miles, passing the Arizona Snowbowl Ski Area turnoff. Continue 1.4 miles, then

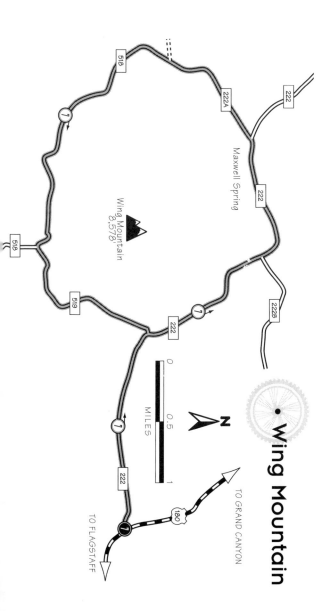

Wing Mountain

TO FLAGSTAFF

TO GRAND CANYON

180

222

MILES
0   0.5   1

N

Wing Mountain
8,578'

518

518

519

222

222

222A

222

222B

Maxwell Spring

35

turn left on Forest Road 222 and park just short of the gate. This turnoff is just a few yards beyond the Experimental Forest turnoff.

The Ride

0.0 Pedal up FR 222, a maintained dirt road; it climbs gradually westward through thick "doghair" stands of young ponderosa pine.

0.8 Wing Mountain is visible ahead.

1.6 Stay right at the junction with FR 519, which will be the return. Aspen trees are visible on the left, flanking the northeast slopes of Wing Mountain. There's a view of the San Francisco Peaks to the northeast. The road levels out as it enters a series of meadows.

2.8 FR 222B branches right; ride straight, staying on FR 222.

3.7 Maxwell Spring is on the left. Turn left (southwest) on FR 222A, which is also a maintained road, though narrower than FR 222. The road leaves the last meadow

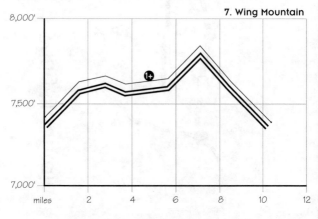

and starts to climb gradually along the west side of Wing Mountain.

5.6   FR 222A goes right; stay left (southeast) on FR 518. Prepare to downshift; the ride's steepest hill is ahead. After climbing a densely forested ravine, the road flattens out to cross a volcanic plateau south of Wing Mountain.

7.1   FR 518 goes right; pedal straight ahead on FR 519. A short, easy ascent to the high point of the ride leads to a long downhill cruise.

8.5   End of loop at FR 222; turn right and coast down the gentle hill.

10.2 US 180 and your starting point.

Tunnel Spring

Location: On the west side of Flagstaff.

Distance: 5.6-mile loop.

Time: 1.5 hours.

Tread: 1 mile on paved streets, 2.9 miles on doubletrack, 1.7 miles on wide singletrack.

Aerobic level: Moderate.

Technical difficulty: 1 on city streets, 3 on doubletrack, 2 on singletrack.

Hazards: Sections of the doubletrack are rocky. Keep your speed down on the urban trail and watch for hikers, runners, and other cyclists.

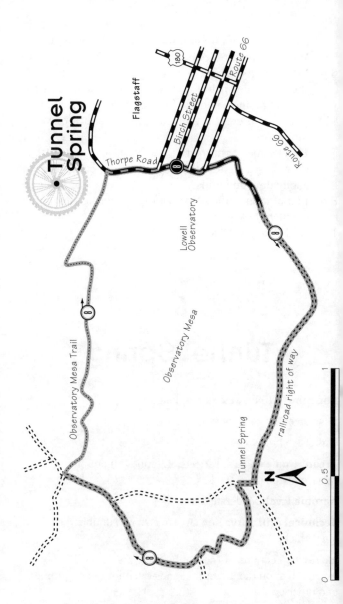

Tunnel Spring

Flagstaff

Route 66

180

Birch Street

Thorpe Road

8

Route 66

Lowell Observatory

8

Observatory Mesa

Observatory Mesa Trail

8

railroad right of way

Tunnel Spring

8

N

0   0.5   1

Highlights: This is a short but interesting loop accessible from Flagstaff. The return is a downhill cruise on smooth, wide singletrack.

Land status: Coconino National Forest, private.

Maps: USGS Flagstaff West; Coconino National Forest.

Access: From the junction of U.S. Highway 180 and Route 66 in west Flagstaff, drive 2 blocks north on US 180 (Humphreys Street), then turn left on Birch Avenue. Go 7 blocks to Thorpe Road, cross the street, and park near the tennis courts on the left, opposite the Adult Center.

The Ride

0.0 From the corner of Birch and Thorpe, pedal 2 blocks south on Thorpe, then go left on Santa Fe Avenue. Turn right onto Sycamore Street. Continue a couple of blocks, where the street becomes Lower Coconino Avenue. Follow this street around a right turn and west to its dead end.

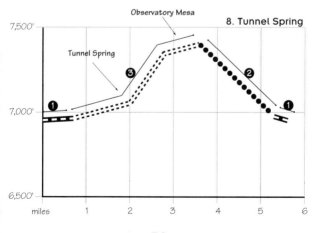

0.7	Pedal through an open gate and onto the doubletrack along the railroad right-of-way. Follow this somewhat rocky road west along the tracks.
2.0	Go right through a wire gate, ride past Tunnel Springs (a stock tank that is often dry), and start cranking up the hill. There are several confusing old roads; stay on the main one, which heads up a draw but then switchbacks to the right.
2.8	The steep climb moderates and the old road becomes smoother as it reaches the top of Observatory Mesa.
3.6	Turn right (east) onto the start of the Observatory Mesa Urban Trail, which is signed for Thorpe Park. The trail passes through private land owned by Lowell Observatory; please stay on the main trail. The smooth, wide singletrack winds through the forest then descends steeply off the mesa.
5.3	Turn right on Thorpe Road and pedal back to Birch Street.
5.6	Corner of Birch and Thorpe and the end of the ride.

Abineau Canyon

Location: 9 miles north of Flagstaff, on the San Francisco Peaks.

Distance: 27 miles out and back.

Time: 5 hours.

Tread: 17.4 miles on maintained, narrow dirt road; 9.6 miles on doubletrack.

Aerobic level: Moderate.

Technical difficulty: 2+.

Hazards: Snow may block the north-facing slopes of this ride until May or early June. Be alert for City of Flagstaff and Forest Service vehicles on Waterline Road. This ride follows a corridor through the Kachina Peaks Wilderness. Stay on the road to avoid entering the wilderness, which is closed to bicycles.

Highlights: The highest, most alpine ride in this guide, with views of the Grand Canyon and the north slopes of Humphreys Peak, the highest point in the state. Fall colors are spectacular on this ride.

Land status: Coconino National Forest.

Maps: USGS Humphreys Peak, Sunset Crater West; Coconino National Forest.

Access: From the junction of Route 66 and U.S. Highway 180 in west Flagstaff, drive 3.2 miles north on US 180, then turn right on the paved Schultz Pass Road (Forest Road 420). Follow this road through a sharp right then left turn, where it

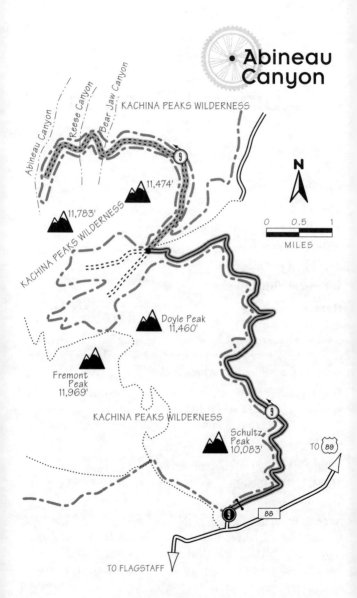

Abineau Canyon

KACHINA PEAKS WILDERNESS

Abineau Canyon

Reese Canyon

Bear Jaw Canyon

KACHINA PEAKS WILDERNESS

11,783'

11,474'

N

0   0.5   1
MILES

KACHINA PEAKS WILDERNESS

Doyle Peak
11,460'

Fremont
Peak
11,969'

KACHINA PEAKS WILDERNESS

Schultz
Peak
10,083'

TO 89

88

TO FLAGSTAFF

becomes dirt. After about 5 miles the road levels out and crosses Schultz Pass. Turn off at the second left, 6.3 miles from US 180 (this unsigned turnoff is east of the Sunset Trailhead). This narrow maintained dirt road is Waterline Road, which is the route used to bring water from the wells and springs in the Inner Basin to Flagstaff. It's closed at a gate 0.7 mile ahead; park at any of several pullouts before reaching the gate.

The Ride

0.0 Go around the gate. The road beyond this point is open only to hikers and cyclists. It climbs gently as it starts around the slopes of Schultz Peak.

2.0 Ride through a short tunnel.

8.7 A trail junction marked by signs and several buildings. The largest cabin is an emergency shelter for snow surveyors, who measure the winter snowpack. In late winter, it's common for it to be buried up to the roof! A spigot near the cabin offers a chance to refill your bottles with untreated mountain spring water. Pedal straight ahead on the Abineau Canyon road, which climbs gradually as it continues around the east ridge of

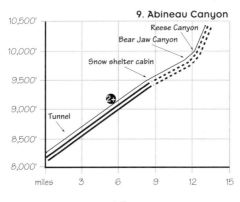

Humphreys Peak. This section of the road is rarely maintained. The spring at the end of the road is dry, and you'll see sections of the abandoned pipeline in the road surface. Please stay on the road, the boundaries of the Kachina Peaks Wilderness are on either side.

11.8 The old road crosses Bear Jaw Canyon, the first of three major canyons on the north side of the mountain.

12.5 Ride around the sharp bend at Reese Canyon. The road becomes steeper and rockier.

13.5 The old road dead ends at Abineau Canyon and the Kachina Peaks Wilderness boundary. This is the end of the ride. The summit of 12,633-foot Humphreys Peak, Arizona's highest, towers 2,600 feet above. The vista down the canyon gives a view of the cliffs of the North Rim of the Grand Canyon, 50 miles away, and part of the Painted Desert. After soaking it all in, turn around and retrace your tracks to the trailhead.

Rocky Ridge

Location: North-central Flagstaff.

Distance: 10.3-mile loop.

Time: 2 hours.

Tread: 7.2 miles on singletrack, 3.1 miles on paved road.

Aerobic level: Moderate.

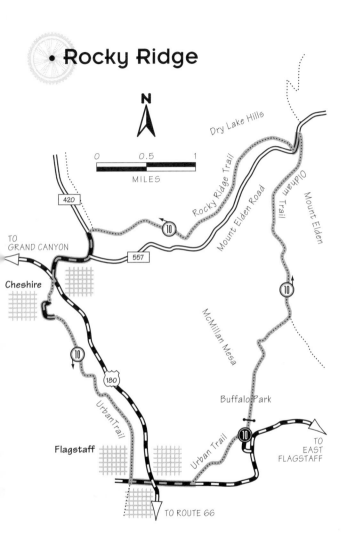

• Rocky Ridge

N

0   0.5   1
MILES

420

Dry Lake Hills

Rocky Ridge Trail

Mount Elden Road

Oldham Trail

Mount Elden

10

TO
GRAND CANYON

557

Cheshire

10

McMillan Mesa

180

Urban Trail

Buffalo Park

10

Flagstaff

Urban Trail

10

TO
EAST
FLAGSTAFF

TO ROUTE 66

Technical difficulty: 1 on roads, 2 on wide singletrack, 3 with sections of 4 on singletrack.

Hazards: This is a popular trail—watch for other riders, hikers, and horses on the singletrack.

Highlights: Scenic views from Buffalo Park, fun singletrack with minimal elevation gain. This loop ride is equally enjoyable in either direction.

Land status: Coconino National Forest, private.

Maps: USGS Flagstaff West, Humphreys Peak, Sunset Crater West; Coconino National Forest.

Access: From the junction of U.S. Highway 180 and Route 66 in west Flagstaff, drive north on US 180 (Humphreys Street), then turn right onto Columbus Avenue at a traffic light. Go 1 block, then turn left on Beaver Street. Turn right on Forest Drive at a traffic light. At the top of the hill, turn left on the

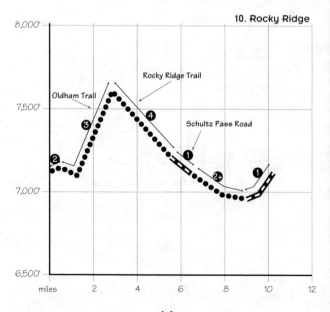

46

signed road for Buffalo Park and the USGS Astrogeology Center. Continue to the end of the road and park.

The Ride

0.0 Ride north on the urban trail through the gate and across Buffalo Park.

0.5 Pedal right on singletrack just before the natural gas pumping station, then through a fence and past a sign for Oldham Trail.

0.7 Follow the singletrack left down the hill—don't follow the wide pipeline right-of-way.

1.0 Ignore the numerous unmarked side trails; go straight.

1.3 Signed junction with Pipeline Trail; ride straight across the pipeline right-of-way to continue on Oldham Trail. The trail starts to climb along the base of Mount Elden.

2.9 Cross dirt Mount Elden Road (Forest Road 557) at a cattleguard and pedal up Rocky Ridge Trail. The trail contours along the base of the Dry Lake Hills.

3.7 Bear right at an unsigned T intersection.

5.6 Signed trailhead shared with the Schultz Creek Trail. Go left on the dirt road.

5.7 Go left on maintained dirt Schultz Pass Road (FR 420), which turns to pavement.

6.5 Ride across busy US 180 (Fort Valley Road) onto a wide singletrack, into the Cheshire subdivision.

6.7 Turn left on Fremont Street.

6.9 Turn left on Lynette Street.

7.0 The street ends; continue on wide singletrack (the city plans to extend the urban trail system through here to Cheshire).

7.6 Bear sharply left on narrow singletrack just before a cindered driveway. Stay to the right of the creek (the Rio de Flag); there are multiple trails.

7.9 Go left on a narrow paved street, which becomes Venus Drive.

8.0 Turn left on Crescent Drive, then join the start of the urban trail next to the Rio de Flag.

8.7 Go left on Anderson Street.

8.8 Take another left on Whipple Road, then lean right on McMillan Road.

9.0 Go left on Beal Road.

9.1 Turn right on busy US 180 (Fort Valley Road), then immediately left on Forest Avenue, and pedal up the steep hill.

9.6 Turn left onto San Francisco Street, then immediately right onto the urban trail.

10.3 Roll into the Buffalo Park parking area and the end of the loop.

Mount Elden Loop

Location: 3 miles north of Flagstaff, at the base of Mount Elden.

Distance: 19.6-mile loop.

Time: 5 hours.

Tread: 0.8 mile on doubletrack, 18.8 miles on singletrack.

Aerobic level: Moderate.

Technical difficulty: 2 on doubletrack, 3 with some sections of 4 on singletrack.

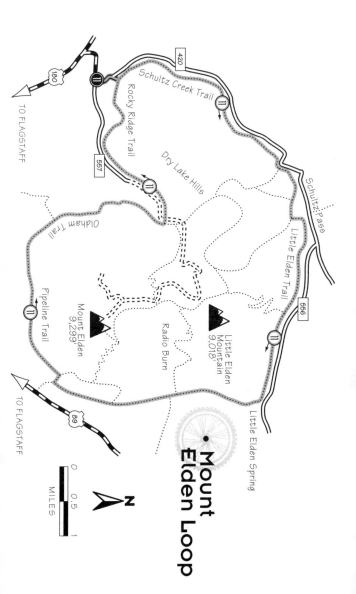

Mount
Elden Loop

TO FLAGSTAFF

180

557

420

Schultz Creek Trail

Rocky Ridge Trail

Dry Lake Hills

Oldham Trail

Pipeline Trail

Mount Elden
9,299'

Radio Burn

Little Elden
Mountain
9,018'

Little Elden Trail

Schultz Pass

556

TO FLAGSTAFF

89

Little Elden Spring

N

MILES
0   0.5   1

Hazards: Heavily used trails—watch for hikers, other cyclists, and horses.

Highlights: Long singletrack loop around the Dry Lake Hills-Mount Elden complex. Mostly smooth trail with technical sections, especially on the Rocky Ridge Trail.

Land status: Coconino National Forest.

Maps: USGS Flagstaff West, Flagstaff East, Humphreys Peak, Sunset Crater West; Coconino National Forest.

Access: From the junction of Route 66 and U.S. Highway 180 in west Flagstaff, drive 3.2 miles north on US 180, then turn right on paved Schultz Pass Road (Forest Road 420). The road turns sharply right, then left at the junction with Mount Elden Road. Park on the right in the dirt parking area. Don't park on the private land to the north.

The Ride

0.0   Turn right onto the Schultz Pass Road, cross a cattleguard, then turn right and coast down a short hill.

0.4   Schultz Creek/Rocky Ridge trailhead. The Rocky Ridge Trail goes right at a sign; it will be the return trail. Continue straight ahead (north) on the signed Schultz Creek Trail. This trail climbs up Schultz Creek (normally dry) around the west side of the Dry Lake Hills. It starts out as old doubletrack but soon becomes smooth singletrack.

1.3   The singletrack becomes somewhat steeper and rockier. The trail follows the route of an old wagon road, the original Schultz Pass Road. You'll see the new Schultz Pass Road just up the hillside to the left.

4.0   Pedal straight ahead at a signed junction with the Schultz Loop Trail (which goes right). The grade eases as the trail comes out onto broad Schultz Pass. Ride east through a parking area, then into a second parking area, for the Sunset Trailhead.

4.5 Ride east on the signed Sunset Trail.

4.8 Turn left (downhill) on Little Elden Trail, skirting the right side of Schultz Tank.

5.0 Turn right (east) on the Little Elden Trail, which soon crosses the creek and climbs slightly as it skirts the slopes of Little Elden Mountain. This section is smooth, fun singletrack, which generally descends.

7.8 Little Elden Spring (a small seep) is in the fenced enclosure to the right. The trail starts to climb and soon enters the Radio Burn, the scar from a devastating human-caused forest fire in 1977.

9.5 Pedal straight ahead at the Heart Trail junction.

9.7 The Sandy Seep Trail branches left; continue straight ahead on the Christmas Tree Trail, which begins to descend gradually.

11.2 Go straight ahead on the Fatmans Loop Trail (the Mount Elden Trail goes right, uphill).

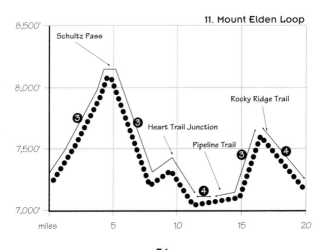

11.4 Pedal right on an unsigned trail, then right again. This short section is steep and technical.

11.5 Go left on the signed Pipeline Trail, which winds through boulders, pines, and oaks as it continues to skirt Mount Elden.

12.2 Ride left (downhill) on the Pipeline Trail.

12.3 Go right on the gas pipeline right-of-way.

13.2 The trail veers right and leaves the gas pipeline for a short distance. Numerous trails cross at right angles; stay on the main trail.

14.8 Junction with Oldham Trail; turn right and follow the singletrack back into the woods above the gas pipeline right-of-way. The riding becomes more technical as the trail starts to climb.

16.4 Cross the dirt Mount Elden Road and start on the signed Rocky Ridge Trail, which is the most technical section of the ride. (If you're hammered, you can turn left and cruise 3 miles down the road to your car.) There are ups and downs, but generally the trail descends along the slopes of the Dry Lake Hills.

19.2 Schultz Creek/Rocky Ridge trailhead. Turn left and follow the doubletrack up to the Schultz Pass Road, then turn left again.

19.6 The parking area.

Dry Lakes

Location: 8 miles north of Flagstaff, in the Dry Lake Hills.

Distance: 5.7-mile loop.

Time: 1.5 hours.

Tread: 5.7 miles on singletrack.

Aerobic level: Moderate.

Technical difficulty: 3.

Hazards: Heavily used trails with hikers and horses, short rocky sections.

Highlights: Scenic, forested loop with views of Mount Elden and the San Francisco Peaks.

Land status: Coconino National Forest, private.

Maps: USGS Humphreys Peak, Sunset Crater West; Coconino National Forest.

Access: From the junction of Route 66 and U.S. Highway 180 in west Flagstaff, drive 3.2 miles north on US 180, then turn right on paved Schultz Pass Road (Forest Road 420). Follow this road through a sharp right then left turn, where it becomes dirt. After 5 miles, turn right at the signed Sunset Trailhead and park.

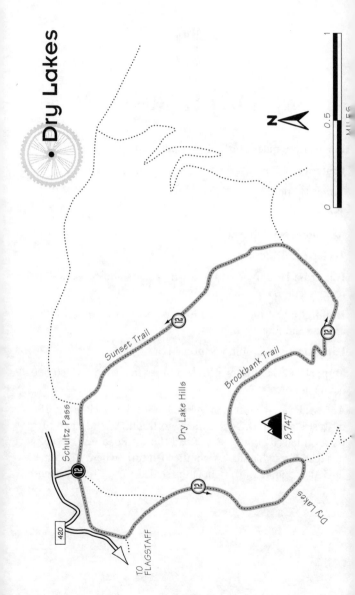

Dry Lakes

N

MILES

0   0.5   1

Schultz Pass

Sunset Trail

Dry Lake Hills

Brookbank Trail

8,747'

Dry Lakes

TO
FLAGSTAFF

420

12

12

12

12

The Ride

0.0   Sunset Trailhead. Pedal west on the Schultz Creek Trail. The smooth singletrack descends into a drainage and soon parallels the Schultz Pass Road.

0.5   Bear sharply left at a gate onto the Schultz Loop Trail, which starts climbing the north side of the Dry Lake Hills.

0.9   Go right (the Schultz Loop Trail goes left) on the old road, now wide singletrack.

1.5   Just as you ride into a meadow, turn left onto well-traveled singletrack. This trail skirts the meadow, one of the Dry Lakes. Part of the meadow sometimes forms a shallow lake right after snowmelt, in April or May. After the meadow, the trail starts to descend and becomes rocky.

1.8   Grunt left on the signed Brookbank Trail, which starts to climb steeply but soon moderates to traverse along the north side of the Dry Lake Hills. There are views of Fremont, Schultz, and Doyle peaks to the north. The trail passes through a couple of meadows then climbs more steeply.

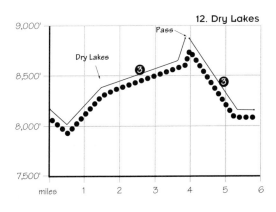

3.9   Go left on the Sunset Trail at a signed junction.

4.0   Ride over a broad pass at the crest of the Dry Lake Hills. It's all downhill from here!

5.3   Go straight at a signed junction with the Little Elden Trail.

5.7   Sunset Trailhead.

Little Bear Trail

Location: 8 miles north of Flagstaff, in the Dry Lake Hills.

Distance: 7.8-mile loop.

Time: 1.5 hours.

Tread: 7.8 miles on singletrack.

Aerobic level: Moderate.

Technical difficulty: 3.

Hazards: Heavily used trails with lots of other riders, hikers, and some horses.

Highlights: A very scenic ride on mostly smooth singletrack.

Land status: Coconino National Forest.

Maps: USGS Humphreys Peak, Sunset Crater West; Coconino National Forest.

Access: From the junction of Route 66 and U.S. Highway 180 in west Flagstaff, drive 3.2 miles north on US 180, then turn right on the paved Schultz Pass Road. Follow this road through

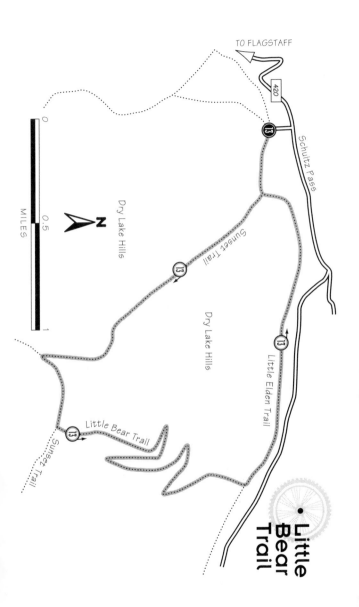

TO FLAGSTAFF

420

Schultz Pass

Dry Lake Hills

N

MILES
0   0.5   1

Sunset Trail

13

Dry Lake Hills

Little Elden Trail

13

Sunset Trail

13

Little Bear Trail

Little Bear Trail

a sharp right then left turn, where it becomes dirt. After 5 miles, turn right at the signed Sunset Trailhead.

The Ride

0.0 Ride east on Sunset Trail.

0.3 Pass the junction with Little Elden Trail, which is the return route. Stay right on Sunset Trail. The smooth singletrack begins to climb steadily through fir, pine, and aspen forest.

1.1 Pedal across a road.

1.5 Crank on up to the ridge at the crest of Dry Lake Hills. Look behind you for great views of the San Francisco Peaks, then cruise down the far side of the ridge.

1.7 Hang a sharp left to stay on Sunset Trail, at the junction with Brookbank Trail.

2.0 Roll out into a meadow at the pass between Dry Lake Hills and Mount Elden. Turn left on Little Bear Trail and start downhill to the north. This fine singletrack descends gradually through three broad switchbacks. It has nice views and only a few technical spots. Keep your speed down and watch for hikers and horses.

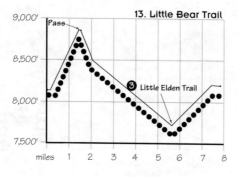

5.7 At the foot of the mountain turn left (west) on Little Elden Trail. The singletrack climbs gradually as it skirts the base of the slope.

7.5 Go right on Sunset Trail to close the loop.

7.8 Sunset Trailhead and the end of the ride.

SP Mountain

Location: About 23 miles north of Flagstaff, in the San Francisco Volcanic Field.

Distance: 20 miles out and back.

Time: 3 hours.

Tread: 20 miles on doubletrack.

Aerobic level: Moderate (the entire ride is easy except the last 0.5 miles to the viewpoint, which is strenuous).

Technical difficulty: 2.

Hazards: If you do the ride in summer, bring lots of water.

Highlights: An easy cruise to a classic volcano. SP Mountain is one of the most symmetric cinder cones in the world. Though the last 0.5 mile to the viewpoint is very steep, this section can be walked, or the volcano can be viewed from its base. An optional side trip takes you to the SP Lava Flow, a 5-mile long field of jagged rock that poured out of the base of SP Mountain. Family groups and others desiring a shorter ride can drive part way up the road.

SP Mountain

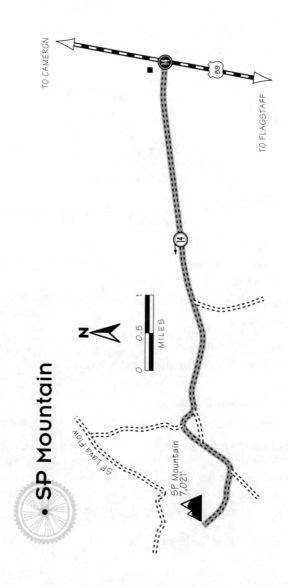

TO CAMERON

14

89

TO FLAGSTAFF

14

N

0   0.5   1
MILES

SP Lava Flow

SP Mountain
7,021'

Land status: State of Arizona, private.

Maps: USGS SP Mountain, East of SP Mountain.

Access: From Flagstaff, drive north on U.S. Highway 89. Note your mileage at Townsend-Winona Road (the last traffic light), then continue 22.8 miles. Turn left on an unsigned road just before a trading post, and park.

The Ride

0.0 Cruise west on the smooth doubletrack. SP Mountain is visible ahead; it's the symmetric hill with a flat top. At each road junction, keep heading toward the mountain.

4.1 Stay right on the main road.

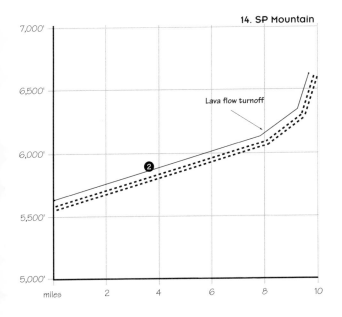

5.8   Pedal straight.

6.3   Bear right to stay on the main road.

7.8   Go right.

8.1   Turn left and ride up the hill (the right fork goes to the lava flow).

8.9   Bear right on the main road.

9.0   Turn right on a doubletrack toward the left side of SP Mountain.

9.5   Start a steep climb. Near the top, the road forks; go left to reach the best viewpoint.

10.0 Viewpoint on a hill next to SP Mountain. SP is 800 feet high and has a 400-foot deep crater. SP Lava Flow is visible to the northeast. Enjoy the views, then return to your car by the same route.

Optional side trip to SP Lava Flow: At the 8.1-mile point, turn right, toward the north side of SP Mountain. Pedal 1.3 miles to the base of the lava flow.

Strawberry Crater

Location: 14 miles north of Flagstaff, northeast of the San Francisco Peaks.

Distance: 11.6 miles out and back.

Time: 2 hours.

Tread: 11.6 miles on doubletrack.

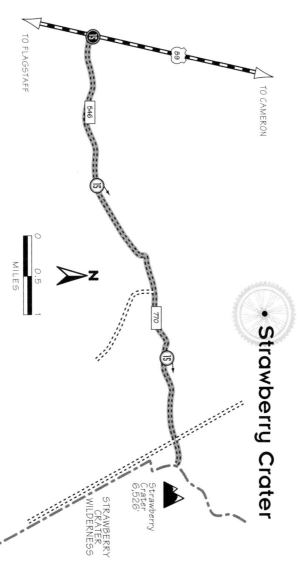

Strawberry Crater

TO FLAGSTAFF

TO CAMERON

89

15

546

15

770

15

N

0   0.5   1

MILES

Strawberry
Crater
6,526'

STRAWBERRY
CRATER
WILDERNESS

Aerobic level: Easy.

Technical difficulty: 2.

Hazards: This can be a warm ride in summer; bring plenty of water. Strawberry Crater itself is part of the Strawberry Crater Wilderness, which is closed to bicycles.

Highlights: The ride starts in pinyon-juniper forest, then winds through tall stands of ponderosa pines to Strawberry Crater, a steep sided, heavily eroded volcano at the southwest edge of a stark lava flow. The crater and lava flow are interesting to explore on foot (bring a bike lock if you plan to do this). Driving the first section can shorten the ride, if desired.

Land status: Coconino National Forest.

Maps: USGS O'Leary Peak, Strawberry Crater; Coconino National Forest.

Access: From Flagstaff, drive north on U.S. Highway 89. Note your mileage at Townsend-Winona Road (the last traffic light), then continue 14 miles. Turn right on an unsigned road (Forest Road 546), and park.

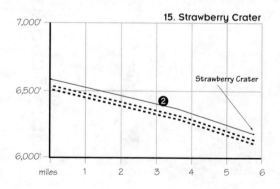

The Ride

0.0   Ride east on the smooth road (FR 546). After about 1 mile, you'll skirt the base of O'Leary Mountain, then climb gradually into ponderosa pine forest.

3.7   Go straight onto FR 770 at this junction.

5.8   Turn-around point at Strawberry Crater. The area east of the powerline is part of the Strawberry Crater Wilderness, and is closed to all vehicles, including bikes. It's a fascinating area to explore on foot.

Grand Falls

Location: About 18 miles northeast of Flagstaff, on the Little Colorado River in the Painted Desert.

Distance: 18.6 miles out and back.

Time: 4 hours.

Tread: 17.6 miles on occasionally maintained dirt road, 1 mile on doubletrack.

Aerobic level: Moderate.

Technical difficulty: 2.

Hazards: Washboards and loose cinders, occasional rocky sections.

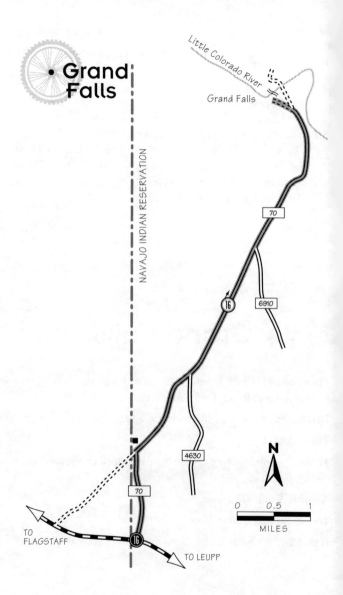

Grand Falls

Little Colorado River

Grand Falls

NAVAJO INDIAN RESERVATION

70

16

6910

4630

70

16

N

0   0.5   1
MILES

TO
FLAGSTAFF

16

TO LEUPP

Highlights: This is a scenic ride though the Painted Desert to a seasonal waterfall on the Little Colorado River. The best time of year to see the falls is in late spring during the snow runoff from eastern Arizona's White Mountains. Try to time your ride for early morning, when the low angle light brings out the pastel colors of the sedimentary rock.

Land status: Navajo Indian Reservation.

Maps: USGS Grand Falls, Grand Falls SW.

Access: From Flagstaff, drive east on Interstate 40 to the Winona Exit, then turn left on paved Fort Townsend-Winona Road. Go 2.1 miles, then turn right on paved Leupp Road. Continue 14.3 miles to the boundary of the Navajo Indian Reservation and the signed turnoff to Grand Falls Bible Church. Park here.

The Ride

0.0 Ride north down a gentle hill on the dirt road, Navajo Route 70. Though the road is maintained, the tread condition varies and the surface may be covered with loose cinders, gouged with deep ruts, and washboarded. A somewhat steeper descent takes you into a broad valley.

1.5 Curve right past the Grand Falls Bible Church, and resume a gentle rate of descent.

3.7 Navajo Route 4630, a maintained dirt road, merges from the right. Note this junction for the return. You're riding down a shallow valley—note the thin veneer of black cinders over the red surface of the road. On the right, the underlying sedimentary rock outcrops as low red ledges. On the left, you can see a dark layer of volcanic rock, remaining from one of the many lava flows that once spread over the area.

7.6 Another maintained dirt road, Navajo Route 6910, merges from the right.

8.8 Turn left on an unmarked doubletrack. If you miss this obscure turnoff, you'll reach a ford across the Little Colorado River at 9.1 miles. The broad riverbed may be nearly dry, or may be roaring with the muddy brown waters of the spring snowmelt. In either case, backtrack 0.3 mile to the unmarked doubletrack. Actually, any of the roads leading west will take you to your goal.

9.3 A number of intersecting doubletracks confuse the last 0.5 mile of the ride. Watch for the small shelters at the overlook and ride toward them. You'll pedal right up to the rim of the river gorge. The river makes a right angle turn to the north after it goes over the falls. For the best view, ride along the left bank and down to the lower overlook facing the falls. As high as Niagara Falls, Grand Falls varies from an insignificant trickle during the dry season to a roaring, muddy torrent during the spring snowmelt. The falls were formed when a lava flow poured into the canyon and diverted the river to

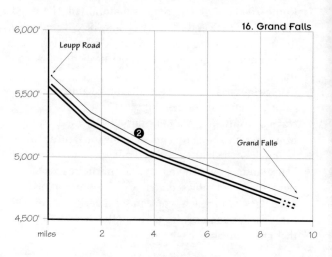

the east. The river made its way around the flow and poured back into the canyon over its east rim. You rode across the lava flow during the last part of the ride, and the lava plug filling the canyon is clearly visible from the lower overlook. From here, retrace your tracks to the beginning.

Walnut Canyon

Location: Flagstaff and Walnut Canyon.

Distance: 23.6 miles out and back.

Time: 3 to 4 hours.

Tread: 11.4 miles on doubletrack, 12.2 miles on singletrack.

Aerobic level: Moderate.

Technical difficulty: 2 on doubletrack, 3+ on singletrack.

Hazards: Deep ruts on doubletrack, rocky and steep sections on singletrack.

Highlights: This ride takes you across a section of the Arizona Trail along the north side of Walnut Canyon. It features lots of smooth single- and doubletrack.

Land status: Coconino National Forest.

Maps: USGS Flagstaff West, Flagstaff East; Coconino National Forest.

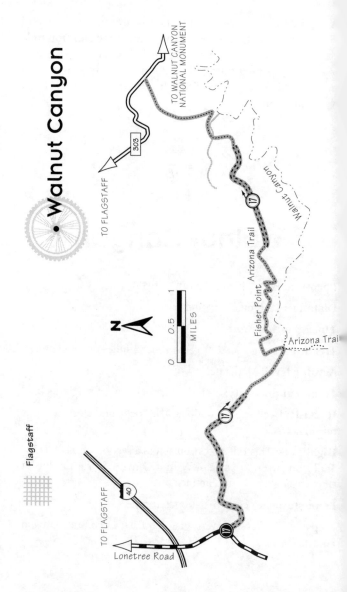

Walnut Canyon

Flagstaff

N

MILES
0   0.5   1

TO FLAGSTAFF

303

TO FLAGSTAFF

TO WALNUT CANYON
NATIONAL MONUMENT

Walnut Canyon

Fisher Point Arizona Trail

Arizona Trail

17

17

17

40

Lonetree Road

Access: From the intersection of Route 66 (Business 40) and Humphreys Street (U.S. Highway 180) in west Flagstaff, drive east 1 block on Route 66, then turn right (south) on Beaver Street. Turn left on Butler Avenue at the traffic light. Next, turn right at a traffic light onto Lone Tree Road. Go south 1.8 miles, where Lone Tree Road makes a sharp right turn, and continue straight ahead onto the dirt road and park.

The Ride

0.0   Ride south on the dirt road and go through a gate onto doubletrack. There are numerous minor forks in this area; stay on the main doubletrack.

1.5   Pass through a gate at the entrance to Walnut Canyon Recreation Area.

3.0   Turn right (southeast) onto singletrack, and descend into a canyon.

3.9   The canyon opens out into a meadow on the floor of Walnut Canyon. Pedal left on the Arizona Trail.

4.0   Hang a sharp left to follow the Arizona Trail up a side canyon and out of Walnut Canyon. (The trail down Walnut Canyon is closed to bikes.) This climb becomes steep and rocky in places.

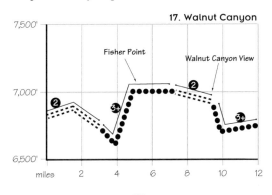

71

4.9   Follow the singletrack right to Fisher Point.

5.0   Walk to the edge of Fisher Point, which overlooks Walnut Canyon, then ride back to the main trail.

5.1   Go right on the Arizona Trail, which closely follows the rim of Walnut Canyon.

6.3   The trail wanders away from the canyon rim to avoid a side canyon.

7.1   Pedal right on doubletrack signed for the Arizona Trail at a confusing intersection. Numerous old roads intersect the trail beyond this point; always follow the Arizona Trail signs and stay on the main doubletrack.

9.4   Go straight on doubletrack to a viewpoint, then backtrack.

9.9   Descend to cross a side canyon. There are a few rocky, steep sections on the descent and the climb up the far side.

11.8 Turn-around point at Old Walnut Canyon Road (Forest Road 303). Follow the route back to the start.

Option: Do the ride one way with a car shuttle. To reach the Walnut Canyon trailhead from Flagstaff, drive east on Interstate 40 to the Walnut Canyon National Monument exit, and go right (south). Just before entering the monument, turn right on Old Walnut Canyon Road (FR 303). Continue 1.8 miles to the Arizona Trail parking area.

Marshall Lake

Location: Southeast of Flagstaff at Walnut Canyon and Marshall Lake.

Distance: 18.8 miles out and back.

Time: 4 hours.

Tread: 6 miles on doubletrack, 12.8 miles on singletrack.

Aerobic level: Easy, with one moderate climb.

Technical difficulty: 2 on doubletrack, 3 on singletrack.

Hazards: Heavily used trail.

Highlights: Scenic Walnut Canyon, good wildlife viewing at Marshall Lake, and smooth double- and singletrack.

Land status: Coconino National Forest, private.

Maps: USGS Flagstaff West, Flagstaff East, Lower Lake Mary; Coconino National Forest.

Access: From the junction of U.S. Highway 180 and Route 66 in west Flagstaff, go east 1 block on Route 66, then turn right (south) on Beaver Street. Go 4 blocks, then turn left on Butler Avenue. Go east 5 blocks, then turn left (south) on Lone Tree Road. The street crosses under the Interstate 40 bridges, then makes a sharp right at the bottom of a hill. Go straight again onto the dirt and park.

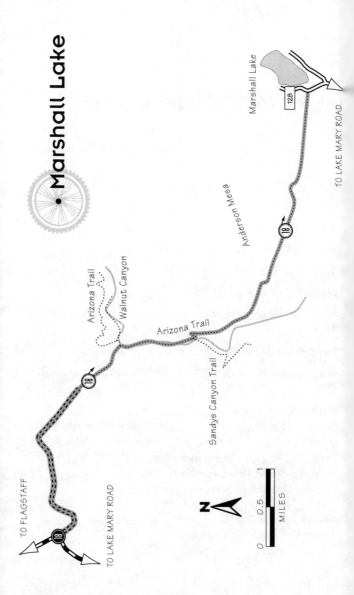

Marshall Lake

Marshall Lake

Anderson Mesa

Arizona Trail

Walnut Canyon

Arizona Trail

Sandys Canyon Trail

TO LAKE MARY ROAD

TO FLAGSTAFF

TO LAKE MARY ROAD

N

0   0.5   1

MILES

74

The Ride

0.0   Ride south on the dirt road and go through a gate onto doubletrack. There are numerous minor forks in this area; stay on the main doubletrack.

1.5   Pass through a gate at the entrance to Walnut Canyon Recreation Area.

3.0   Turn right (southeast) onto singletrack, and descend into a canyon.

3.9   The canyon opens out into a meadow on the floor of Walnut Canyon. Pedal straight ahead to follow the Arizona Trail south up Walnut Canyon.

4.8   The Sandys Canyon Trail goes straight ahead; pedal left on the Arizona Trail, and start a grunt ascent out of Walnut Canyon.

6.0   Whew! Top of the climb. The trail stays on the top of Anderson Mesa, occasionally crossing small drainages as it winds through open pine-oak forest.

9.4   The turn-around point at Marshall Lake Trailhead. The lake is a few hundred yards to the left (east). Usually

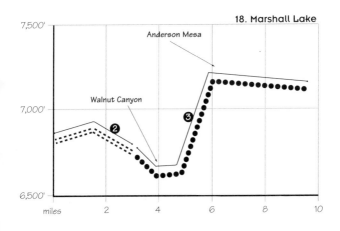

Marshall Lake is a shallow marsh—it's a great place to see wildlife, especially around dawn and dusk.

Option: Do a car shuttle and ride one way. To reach the Marshall Lake Trailhead from Flagstaff at the junction of Route 66 and US 180, drive south on South Milton Road, then turn right at a traffic light onto Forest Meadows Road. After 1 block, turn left onto Beulah Boulevard. Next, turn left onto Lake Mary Road (Forest Highway 3) at a traffic light. Continue about 10.4 miles, then turn left onto Marshall Lake Road (Forest Road 128). When this paved road reaches the top of Anderson Mesa, turn left onto a maintained dirt road (FR 128). In another 0.8 mile the road forks; go left 0.2 mile to the Arizona Trail parking area.

Hidden Cabin

Location: About 23 miles south of Flagstaff on the Mogollon Rim.

Distance: 17.8 miles out and back.

Time: 3 hours.

Tread: 11.6 miles on maintained dirt road, 6.2 miles on doubletrack.

Aerobic level: Moderate.

Technical difficulty: 2 on maintained dirt road, 2+ on doubletrack.

• Hidden Cabin

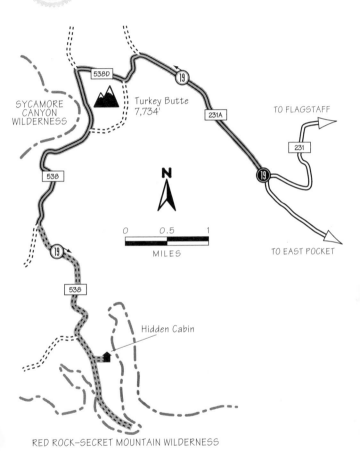

SYCAMORE
CANYON
WILDERNESS

538D

Turkey Butte
7,734'

TO FLAGSTAFF

19

231A

231

538

19

N

19

538

0   0.5   1
MILES

Hidden Cabin

TO EAST POCKET

RED ROCK–SECRET MOUNTAIN WILDERNESS

Hazards: The usual ruts and rocks on the doubletrack section.

Highlights: You'll see a historic cabin, and views of Secret Mountain and Loy Canyon from the Mogollon Rim on this forest cruise.

Land status: Coconino National Forest.

Maps: USGS Dutton Hill, Sycamore Point, Loy Butte; Coconino National Forest.

Access: From Flagstaff at the junction of West Route 66 and South Milton Road, drive 2 miles west on West Route 66, then turn south on paved Woody Mountain Road (Forest Road 231). After 1 mile, the road becomes maintained dirt. Continue another 19.9 miles to the junction with FR 231A, and park.

The Ride

0.0 Start by pedaling west on FR 231A, a maintained dirt road, which climbs gradually as it follows a drainage.

2.6 Hang a right on FR 538D.

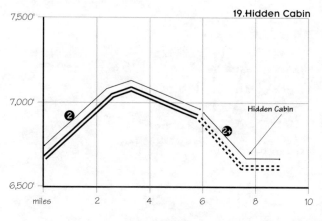

3.3   Go left on FR 538.
5.8   Stay left on FR 538, a doubletrack.
7.5   Turn left at an unsigned junction.
7.8   Go left on a side road to visit Hidden Cabin.
7.9   Hidden Cabin was probably built as a line shack by sheep herders and cattlemen, like several other cabins in this area.
8.0   Return to the main road.
8.7   Walk a few yards southwest from the road for good views of upper Loy Canyon.
8.9   Secret Mountain Trailhead and the end of the ride. You are on the edge of the Mogollon Rim, which is the boundary of the Red Rock-Secret Mountain Wilderness (no bikes!). The Secret Mountain Trail drops into the saddle between Secret and Loy canyons before climbing onto Secret Mountain. Secret Cabin, another historic fire guard structure, is about 1.5 miles south on the trail. Bring a bike lock if you intend to do this hike.

Bear Sign Canyon Overlook

Location: About 30 miles south of Flagstaff on the Mogollon Rim.

Distance: 7 miles out and back.

Time: 2 hours.

Tread: 7 miles on doubletrack.

Aerobic level: Easy.

Technical difficulty: 2.

Hazards: There are some rocky and rutted sections.

Highlights: An easy ride through magnificent ponderosa pine forest to a fine viewpoint on the Mogollon Rim, overlooking Bear Sign Canyon.

Land status: Coconino National Forest.

Maps: USGS Wilson Mountain; Coconino National Forest.

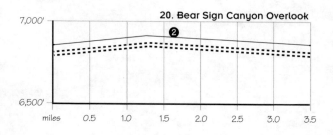

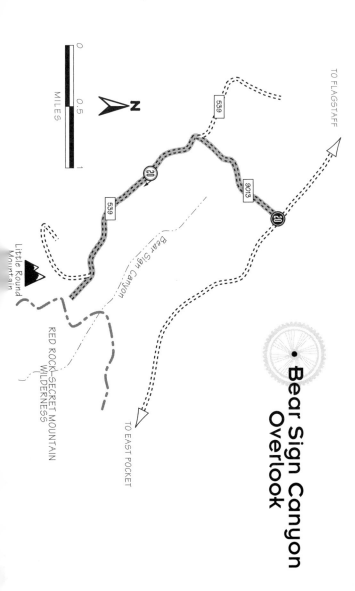

Bear Sign Canyon
Overlook

TO FLAGSTAFF

TO EAST POCKET

RED ROCK–SECRET MOUNTAIN
WILDERNESS

Little Round
Mountain

Bear Sign Canyon

539

539

9013

20

20

N

MILES

0

0.5

1

Access: From Flagstaff at the junction of West Route 66 and South Milton Road, drive 2 miles west on West Route 66, then turn south on paved Woody Mountain Road (Forest Road 231). After 1 mile, the road becomes maintained dirt. Continue another 26 miles to the junction with FR 9013, a doubletrack on the right, and park.

The Ride

0.0 Ride south on FR 9013 through ponderosa pine forest.
0.4 Stay right.
0.9 Bear left and pedal up a gradual climb.
1.3 Turn left at the junction with FR 539.
3.1 Stay left.
3.5 You're on the Mogollon Rim at the edge of Red Rock-Secret Mountain Wilderness overlooking Bear Sign Canyon. There are several viewpoints here, each offering a slightly different view of this wild canyon. The wilderness itself is closed to bicycles. Retrace your tracks to the beginning.

East Pocket

Location: About 30 miles south of Flagstaff on the Mogollon Rim.

Distance: 7.8 miles out and back.

Time: 2 hours.

Tread: 7.8 miles on doubletrack.

Aerobic level: Easy.

Technical difficulty: 2.

Hazards: Of course, there are a few rocky and rutted sections along the doubletrack.

Highlights: Another easy ride to a Mogollon Rim viewpoint; this one overlooks the head of Dry Creek in the East Pocket area. As an option, you can explore numerous side roads that lead to views of West Fork Oak Creek and other canyons.

Land status: Coconino National Forest.

Maps: USGS Wilson Mountain; Coconino National Forest.

Access: From Flagstaff at the junction of West Route 66 and South Milton Road, drive 2 miles west on West Route 66, then turn south on paved Woody Mountain Road (Forest Road 231). After 1 mile, the road becomes maintained dirt. Continue another 26 miles to the junction with FR 9013, a doubletrack on the right, and park.

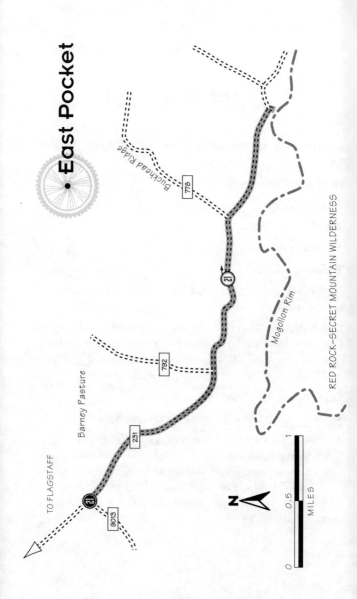

East Pocket

RED ROCK–SECRET MOUNTAIN WILDERNESS

Buckhead Ridge

Mogollon Rim

Barney Pasture

TO FLAGSTAFF

778

792

231

9013

N

MILES

0   0.5   1

The Ride

0.0   Pedal east on FR 231, the main road, which climbs gradually though ponderosa pine forest and meadows.

1.4   Continue straight past the junction with FR 792 and start a very gradual descent.

2.7   Again, go straight as you roll past the junction with FR 778.

3.8   Take a short spur road on the right to reach the viewpoint.

3.9   The view from the Mogollon Rim encompasses the head of Dry Creek and the red rock formations near Sedona, part of the Red Rock-Secret Mountain Wilderness. The rim is the wilderness boundary; the land beyond is closed to bicycles. East Pocket is the low hill on the rim to the southeast. Locally, "pocket" is used to describe a mesa surrounded by a rim on three sides.

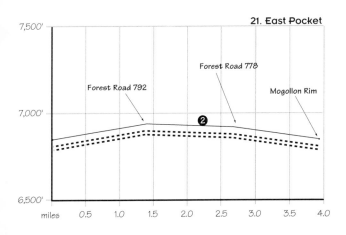

21. East Pocket

Fry Park

Location: About 14 miles south of Flagstaff on the Coconino Plateau.

Distance: 13.4 miles out and back (8 miles if the first 2.7 miles are driven).

Time: 3 hours.

Tread: 13.4 miles on maintained dirt road.

Aerobic level: Moderate (easy if the first 2.7 miles are driven).

Technical difficulty: 2.

Hazards: Watch for some deep ruts on the last mile of the ride, especially in spring. The tread becomes very muddy during snow melt and after heavy rain.

Highlights: Except for the moderate but sustained climb at the start, this is an easy ride to an alpine meadow with great wild-flowers in early summer. The climb can be avoided by driving the first 2.7 miles.

Land status: Coconino National Forest.

Maps: USGS Mountainaire, Dutton Hill; Coconino National Forest.

Access: From Flagstaff, drive south on Interstate 17 about 2 miles, then exit onto Arizona Highway 89A toward Sedona. Continue about 11.5 miles to the junction with Fry Park Road (Forest Road 535), and park.

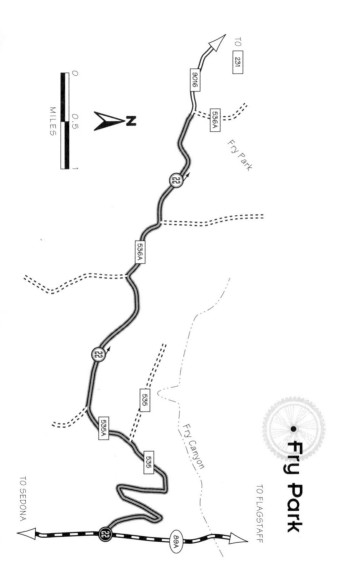

TO 231

536A

Fry Park

22

536A

N

MILES
0   0.5   1

22

535

535A

535

Fry Canyon

TO SEDONA

22

89A

TO FLAGSTAFF

• Fry Park

9016

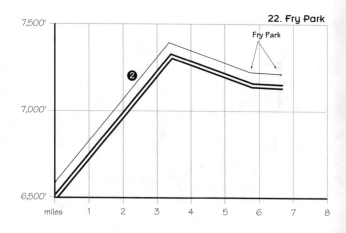

The Ride

0.0 Ride west on FR 535, a maintained dirt road that climbs steadily west up several broad switchbacks.

2.7 You've reached the top of the climb; now pedal left on FR 535A, the main road.

3.4 Bear right to stay on FR 535A.

5.0 Go right on FR 536A, heading west.

5.8 Hang a left and ride along the south side of Fry Park, a former lake bed that is a dry meadow except during snow melt.

6.7 Junction with FR 9016 and the end of the ride at the west end of Fry Park. You can hide your bike or lock it to a tree anywhere along the last mile of the ride, and hike north to explore the park. It's especially fine after a wet spring when the wildflowers are blooming. Ride back to the beginning on the same route you followed in.

Mormon Lake

Location: About 20 miles southeast of Flagstaff at Mormon Lake.

Distance: 16.2-mile loop.

Time: 2 hours.

Tread: 16.2 miles on paved road.

Aerobic level: Easy.

Technical difficulty: 1.

Hazards: Watch for traffic on Mormon Lake Road.

Highlights: Although this ride is entirely on pavement, the ride around Arizona's largest natural lake is so great it just had to be in this book. Mormon Lake varies from a large, shallow lake in the spring to a marsh in late summer. It's a great place to see wildlife.

Land status: Coconino National Forest, private.

Maps: USGS Mormon Lake; Coconino National Forest.

Access: From Flagstaff, drive south on South Milton Road, then turn right at a traffic light onto Forest Meadows Road. After 1 block, turn left onto Beulah Boulevard. Next, turn left onto Lake Mary Road (Forest Highway 3) at a traffic light. Continue 20 miles on this paved road, and park at the north turnoff to Mormon Lake.

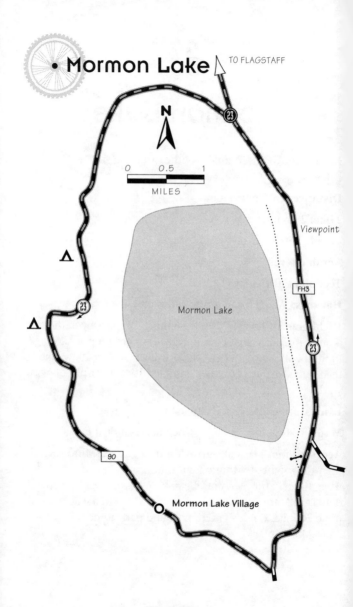

Mormon Lake

TO FLAGSTAFF

N

0   0.5   1
MILES

Viewpoint

FH3

Mormon Lake

90

Mormon Lake Village

The Ride

0.0 Ride west on Mormon Lake Road.

2.7 Cruise across a meadow; the forested hump of Mormon Mountain is visible ahead.

3.4 The road reaches the shore of Mormon Lake and follows it.

7.8 Mormon Lake Village.

9.9 The end of Mormon Lake Road; turn left on Lake Mary Road and cruise down a hill into a meadow at the southwest edge of the lake.

11.4 A short side road leads left to a trailhead. If you have a bike lock, you might want to check out this trail; it follows the east shore of the lake and is a great place to view wildlife. Back on Lake Mary Road, pedal up a short climb to reach the bluffs along the east side of the lake.

14.8 Turn left and go a few yards to a viewpoint overlooking the lake.

16.2 North Mormon Lake Road and the end of the ride.

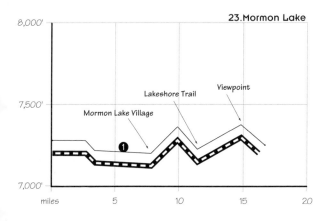

Kinnikinick Lake

Location: About 31 miles southeast of Flagstaff on Anderson Mesa.

Distance: 24.4-mile loop.

Time: 5 hours.

Tread: 4.9 miles on paved road, 10 miles on maintained dirt road, 9.5 miles on doubletrack.

Aerobic level: Moderate.

Technical difficulty: 1 on paved road, 2 on maintained dirt road, 3+ on doubletrack.

Hazards: You might want to walk a couple of very rocky sections along the doubletrack. Otherwise, watch for ruts and occasional rocks.

Highlights: A long ride through a variety of terrain, from ponderosa pine forest to pinyon-juniper woodland to grassy savanna. The destination is a natural lake that was enlarged with a dam.

Land status: Coconino National Forest.

Maps: USGS Hutch Mountain, Kinnikinick Lake, Mormon Lake; Coconino National Forest.

Access: From Flagstaff at the junction of Route 66 and U.S. Highway 180, drive south on South Milton Road, then turn right at a traffic light onto Forest Meadows Road. After a block, turn left onto Beulah Boulevard. Next, turn left onto Lake Mary

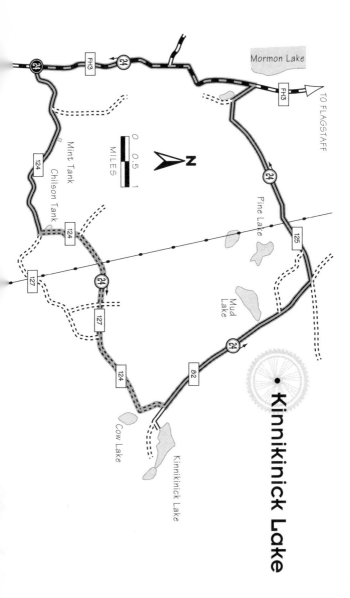

Mormon Lake

FH3

TO FLAGSTAFF

FH3

24

Mint Tank

Chilson Tank

124

124

24

127

127

127

124

Cow Lake

82

Pine Lake

Mud Lake

Kinnikinick Lake

24

MILES

0   0.5   1

N

125

24

• Kinnikinick Lake

Road (Forest Highway 3) at a traffic light. Continue about 29 miles on this paved road, and park at Forest Road 124. This turnoff is in a meadow 3 miles south of the south Mormon Lake Road junction.

The Ride

0.0   Pedal east across the meadow on FR 124, a maintained dirt road.

1.0   Start a climb up a short, moderate hill.

1.8   Cruise past Mint Tank and Mint Spring.

3.9   Ride left to stay on FR 124, which becomes doubletrack and passes Chilson Tank. The old road follows the bed of Kinnikinick Canyon and becomes very rocky in places.

4.3   Stay right, then cross under a double powerline. The tread improves after this point.

5.3   Continue straight ahead.

6.4   Bear right, then turn left on FR 127.

7.0   Go left on FR 124.

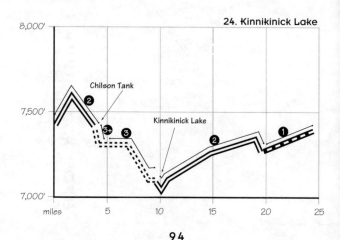

94

8.9 Ride past Cow Lake.

9.5 Junction with Kinnikinick Lake Road (FR 82), a somewhat maintained dirt road. This will be our return, but for now, turn right toward the lake.

9.9 Pedal left to Kinnikinick Campground and the lake.

10.1 Boat launch area and the turnaround point.

10.3 Go right on FR 82 (northwest).

10.7 Ride past FR 124, continuing straight.

13.3 Cruise past Mud Lake.

14.7 Hang a left onto FR 125, and ride southwest; the road surface improves.

15.8 Cross under the double powerlines again.

18.9 Bear right at a minor fork.

19.5 Turn left onto Lake Mary Road, which is paved.

24.4 FR 124 and the end of the ride.

Stoneman Lake

Location: About 36 miles southeast of Flagstaff near the Mogollon Rim.

Distance: 12.2 miles out and back.

Time: 2 hours.

Tread: 12.2 miles on maintained dirt road.

Aerobic level: Easy.

Technical difficulty: 2.

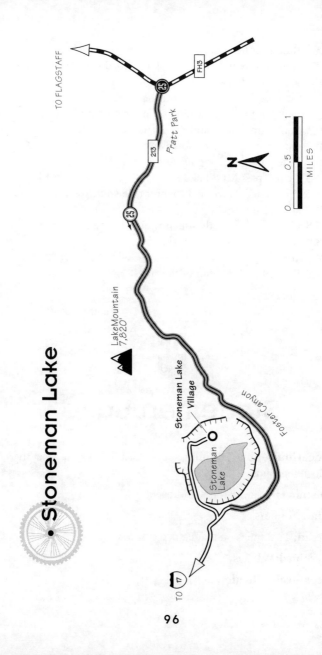

Stoneman Lake

TO FLAGSTAFF

FH3

213

Pratt Park

Lake Mountain
7,820'

Stoneman Lake
Village

Stoneman
Lake

Foster Canyon

TO 17

N

0   0.5   1
MILES

Hazards: Occasional ruts and rocks.

Highlights: An easy ride to a unique, spring-fed mountain lake, set in an unusual depression.

Land status: Coconino National Forest.

Maps: USGS Hutch Mountain, Stoneman Lake; Coconino National Forest.

Access: From Flagstaff, drive south on South Milton Road, then turn right at a traffic light onto Forest Meadows Road. After 1 block, turn left onto Beulah Boulevard. Next, turn left onto Lake Mary Road (Forest Highway 3) at a traffic light. Continue about 34 miles on this paved road, and park at the Stoneman Lake turnoff, Forest Road 213.

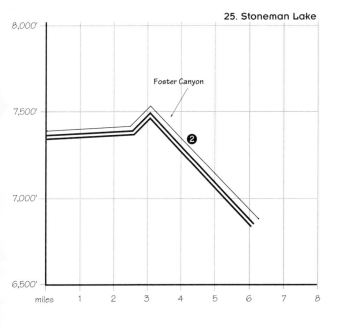

25. Stoneman Lake

The Ride

0.0   Pedal west on the Stoneman Lake Road (FR 213) across Pratt Park, a large meadow.

2.6   Ride along the south edge of a smaller meadow, then start a gradual, short climb.

3.1   Descend southwest into Foster Canyon, then roll down a ridge.

6.1   Turn right at the Stoneman Lake viewpoint. The lake is set in a depression formed in volcanic rocks and is fed by several springs. Oddly, the depression does not appear to be a volcanic crater or caldera, and there's no evidence of a meteor impact. One theory is that faulting led to collapse in the underlying limestone rocks, causing a depression to form. Stoneman Lake is a noted wildlife viewing area and fishing lake; it's one of the few natural lakes in Arizona. After exploring the surroundings on foot, retrace your tracks to the beginning.

Loy Butte

Location: 7 miles west of Sedona below the Mogollon Rim.

Distance: 17 miles out and back.

Time: 4 hours.

Tread: 17 miles on maintained dirt road.

Aerobic level: Easy.

Technical difficulty: 2.

Hazards: Rocks, potholes, and ruts on heavily used road. Conditions vary with weather and the amount of recent maintenance.

Highlights: This ride features scenic red rock views, a natural arch, and an ancient ruin.

Land status: Coconino National Forest, private.

Maps: USGS Wilson Mountain, Loy Butte; Coconino National Forest.

Access: From the junction of Arizona Highway 89A and AZ 179 (the Y) in Sedona, drive west on AZ 89A through west Sedona. When the road starts to curve left, turn right at a traffic light onto Dry Creek Road (Forest Road 152C). Go 5 miles on this paved road, then turn left at the junction with Long Canyon Road, remaining on FR 152C. After another 1.7 miles, the pavement goes sharply right at the junction with dirt Boynton Pass Road (FR 152C). Park here.

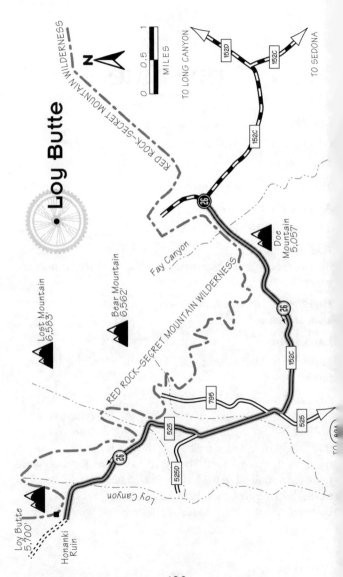

Loy Butte

RED ROCK–SECRET MOUNTAIN WILDERNESS

N

MILES
0   0.5   1

TO LONG CANYON

152D

152C

152C

TO SEDONA

36

Fay Canyon

Doe Mountain
5,057'

36

152C

Lost Mountain
6,583'

Bear Mountain
6,562'

RED ROCK–SECRET MOUNTAIN WILDERNESS

795

525

525

TO 89A

36

525

525D

Loy Canyon

Loy Butte
5,700'

Honanki Ruin

The Ride

).0   Ride southwest on this maintained but sometimes rough dirt road FR 152C. It climbs, dips, and winds through small washes in the pinyon-juniper forest.

).5   Fay Canyon Trailhead is on the right. If you have a bike lock, it's a short and scenic hike to the natural arch, which is well hidden next to a towering cliff.

).9   Pedal up and over Boynton Pass and into a meadow. Doe Mountain is the flat mesa on the left, and Bear Mountain is the large monolith on the right.

1.3   Ride past the Bear Mountain Trailhead on the right. (Both the Bear Mountain and Fay Canyon trails are in the Red Rock-Secret Mountain Wilderness, which is closed to bikes.) The view opens out as you pedal into an open, nearly flat section. The road seems to wander far from the red rocks, but hang in there.

4.0   Hang a right onto Red Canyon Road, FR 525.

4.1   Go left onto Loy Canyon Road, FR 525. You'll ride along a ridge with good views of the Verde Valley to the

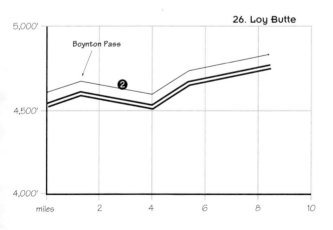

west and southwest, and the cliffs of Bear Mountain t
the northeast.

5.4 Stay right on Loy Canyon Road (FR 525) at the junc
tion with Bradshaw Road (FR 525D). Coast down int
a valley at the base of the cliffs.

7.7 Boundary of the Hancock Ranch and the Loy Canyon
Trailhead. You'll be on private land for the next 0.8
mile—please stay on the main road.

8.1 Go left at the T intersection, where a sign points ou
"Ruins."

8.5 End of the ride at the Honanki Ruin Trailhead, and the
boundary of the Hancock Ranch. The ruins are only a
few hundred yards from the road, and worth checking
out. They're the remains of a small cliff dwelling that
was probably occupied about 800 years ago. Retrace
your tracks to the beginning from here.

Cockscomb Loop

Location: 7 miles west of Sedona below the Mogollon Rim.

Distance: 9.1-mile loop.

Time: 2 hours.

Tread: 2.7 miles on maintained dirt road, 5.9 miles on
doubletrack, 0.5 mile on singletrack.

Aerobic level: Easy.

• Cockscomb Loop

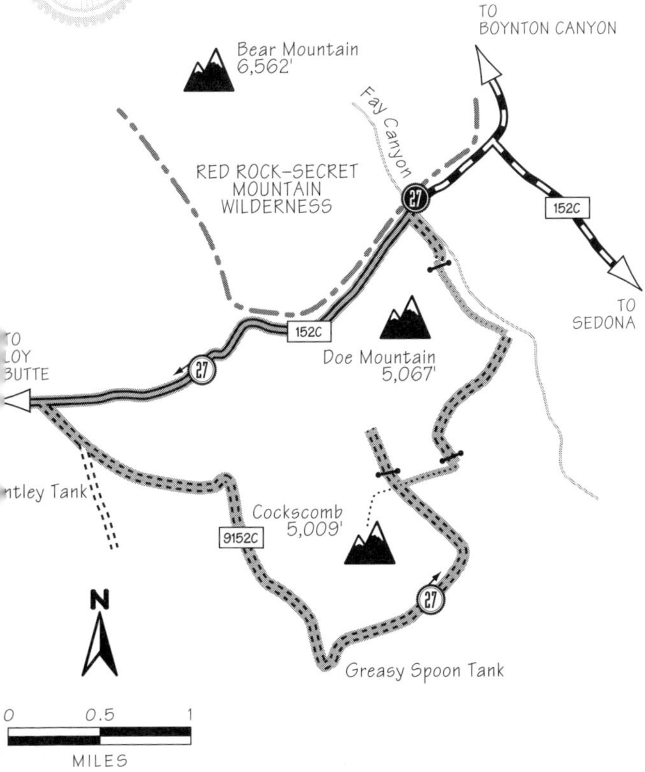

Bear Mountain
6,562'

TO
BOYNTON CANYON

Fay Canyon

RED ROCK–SECRET
MOUNTAIN
WILDERNESS

27

152C

TO SEDONA

152C

27

TO
LOY
BUTTE

Doe Mountain
5,067'

ntley Tank

Cockscomb
5,009'

9152C

27

Greasy Spoon Tank

N

0   0.5   1

MILES

Technical difficulty: 2 on maintained dirt road, 2+ on doubletrack, 3 on singletrack.

Hazards: Heavy traffic on Boynton Pass Road. Watch for horses. Avoid this ride after a heavy rain—it'll be muddy.

Highlights: Easy loop with scenic views of the red rocks near Boynton Pass.

Land status: Coconino National Forest, private.

Maps: USGS Sedona, Loy Butte, Wilson Mountain; Coconino National Forest.

Access: From the junction of Arizona Highway 89A and AZ 179 (the Y) in Sedona, drive west on AZ 89A through west Sedona. When the road starts to curve left, turn right at a traffic light onto Dry Creek Road (Forest Road 152C). Go 5 miles on this paved road, then turn left at the junction with the Long Canyon Road, remaining on FR 152C. After another 1.7 miles, turn left onto dirt Boynton Pass Road (FR 152C). Go another 0.5 mile, then park at the Fay Canyon Trailhead on the right.

The Ride

0.0   Continue on the Boynton Pass Road (FR 152C) as it climbs southwest. Watch for heavy traffic on this maintained but somewhat rocky dirt road.

0.4   Ride over Boynton Pass, and roll downhill through open meadows with great views to the southwest. Bear Mountain towers to the right, and the smaller mass of Doe Mountain is to your left.

2.6   Hang a left on FR 9152C, a rocky, rutted doubletrack that heads slightly downhill to the southeast. You'll be heading toward the right side of the Cockscomb, the serrated red rocks to the right of flat-topped Doe Mountain.

2.9 Stay left after you rumble across a cattleguard and pass Huntley Tank.

5.1 At Greasy Spoon Tank and a corral, go left across a shallow gully and start uphill toward the right side of the Cockscomb. This old doubletrack is badly eroded in places.

5.7 Ride through the pass on the south side of the Cockscomb.

5.8 Pedal right on a well-traveled doubletrack.

5.9 Stay left through an old gate, then right. You want to ride parallel to the base of the Cockscomb, heading generally north.

6.7 At a gate signed "No Trespassing," you'll see a singletrack crossing at right angles. The left trail is a nice hike to the top of the Cockscomb. The ride continues on the right trail, parallel to the fence line; roll downhill on singletrack through the pinyon-juniper forest.

7.0 Go through a wire gate into a (usually) wet area, then turn sharply left, uphill, onto doubletrack. You'll be almost paralleling the fence again, in the opposite direction.

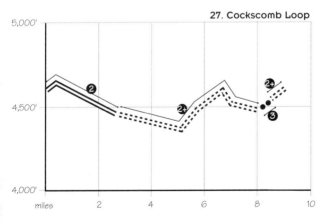

8.0 Go left onto singletrack under the powerline. After passing through a steel gate, go right on doubletrack, then stay generally left, heading northwest toward Bear Mountain.

9.0 Turn right on Boynton Pass Road.

9.1 Go left into the Fay Canyon parking area, and the end of the ride.

Mescal Mountain

Location: About 5 miles west of Sedona in the Boynton Canyon area.

Distance: 4.9-mile loop.

Time: 1 hour.

Tread: 2.4 miles on paved road, 2.5 miles on singletrack.

Aerobic level: Easy.

Technical difficulty: 1 on paved roads, 3- on singletrack.

Hazards: Heavy traffic on paved roads. Watch for horses and hikers on singletrack.

Highlights: Easy loop with fun singletrack through scenic Deadmans Pass.

Land status: Coconino National Forest.

Maps: USGS Wilson Mountain; Coconino National Forest.

• Mescal Mountain

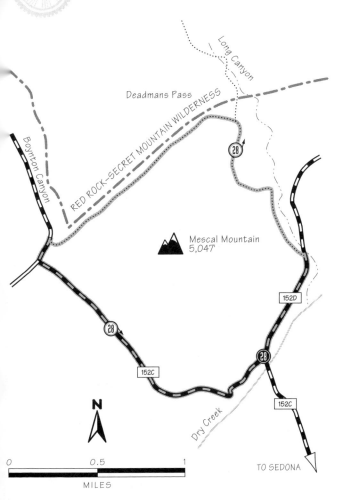

Long Canyon

Deadmans Pass

RED ROCK–SECRET MOUNTAIN WILDERNESS

Boynton Canyon

28

Mescal Mountain
5,047'

152D

28

152C

28

152C

N

Dry Creek

TO SEDONA

0   0.5   1

MILES

Access: From the junction of Arizona Highway 89A and AZ 179 (the Y) in Sedona, drive west on AZ 89A through west Sedona. When the road starts to curve left, turn right at a traffic light onto Dry Creek Road (Forest Road 152C). Go 5 miles on this paved road, then park at the junction with paved Long Canyon Road.

The Ride

0.0 Start by pedaling up paved Long Canyon Road (FR 152D) as it climbs gently through rolling pinyon-juniper woodland.

0.6 Go left onto the Long Canyon Trail, which is easy, wide singletrack. Watch for hikers and horses.

1.7 Turn left again, onto the Deadmans Pass Trail, and climb gradually southwest, paralleling a powerline. (The Long Canyon Trail continues, but goes into the Red Rock-Secret Mountain Wilderness, which is closed to bikes.)

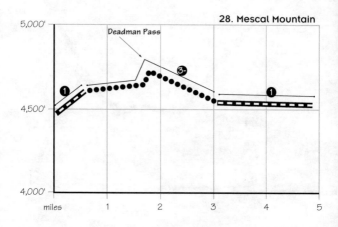

28. Mescal Mountain

1.8 Cross Deadmans Pass and start an enjoyable descent.

2.9 Go right, then left across a wash.

3.1 Hang a left on paved Boynton Canyon Road (FR 152C) and then go left again on paved Boynton Pass Road.

4.9 End of the loop at the junction with Long Canyon Road.

Dry Creek

Location: 2 miles west of Sedona.

Distance: 8.8 miles out and back.

Time: 2 hours.

Tread: 8.8 miles on occasionally maintained dirt road.

Aerobic level: Moderate.

Technical difficulty: 2.

Hazards: Lots of ruts, rocks, and heavy traffic during the summer.

Highlights: Super views of the red rocks and several fine hiking trails. You'll ride through a fine example of Arizona cypress forest—the trees with the curling red bark. If you plan to hike, bring a bike lock. The hiking trails, and the land on either side of the road, are in the Red Rock-Secret Mountain Wilderness, which is closed to bikes.

Land status: Coconino National Forest.

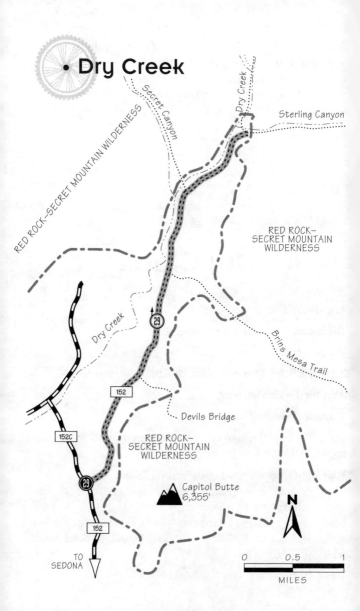

• **Dry Creek**

Secret Canyon

Dry Creek

Sterling Canyon

RED ROCK–SECRET MOUNTAIN WILDERNESS

RED ROCK–
SECRET MOUNTAIN
WILDERNESS

Dry Creek

Brins Mesa Trail

29

152

Devils Bridge

152C

RED ROCK–
SECRET MOUNTAIN
WILDERNESS

29

Capitol Butte
6,355'

N

152

TO
SEDONA

0   0.5   1

MILES

Maps: USGS Wilson Mountain; Coconino National Forest.

Access: From the junction of Arizona Highway 89A and AZ 179 (the Y) in Sedona, drive west on AZ 89A through west Sedona. When the road starts to curve left, turn right at a traffic light onto Dry Creek Road. Go 2.1 miles on this paved road, then turn right on the dirt which becomes Dry Creek Road (Forest Road 152) and park.

The Ride

0.0 FR 152 wanders up and down and around sharp bends. Watch for heavy traffic on this road during the summer. The road surface varies from smooth to rocky and rutted. The towering cliffs of Capitol Butte (known locally as Sugarloaf) tower above you to the right. Pedal north on the dirt road.

1.4 You'll see the Devils Bridge Trailhead on the right. If you have a bike lock, you can sample this and several other great hikes accessible from this ride.

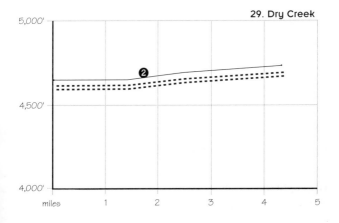

29. Dry Creek

- **2.5** Another parking area on the right marks the Brins Mesa Trailhead.
- **3.5** Watch for a signed trailhead for Secret Canyon on the left. Although the longest hike in the Dry Creek area, it's one of my favorites.
- **4.4** Pedal into a small turn-around loop at the end of the road. From here, trails lead to Vultee Arch, Sterling Pass, and up Bear Sign and Dry Creek canyons in the Red Rock-Secret Mountain Wilderness, which is closed to bikes. The pine-covered ramparts of the Mogollon Rim tower above to the north. When you're done exploring, ride back down to your vehicle.

Jim Thompson Trail

Location: 1 mile north of Sedona.

Distance: 4.6 miles out and back.

Time: 1 hour.

Tread: 4.6 miles on singletrack.

Aerobic level: Moderate.

Technical difficulty: 3.

Hazards: Rocky sections of trail. Keep your speed down and watch for other riders, as well as horses and hikers.

Highlights: Short but fun singletrack ride out to a viewpoint overlooking lower Oak Creek Canyon.

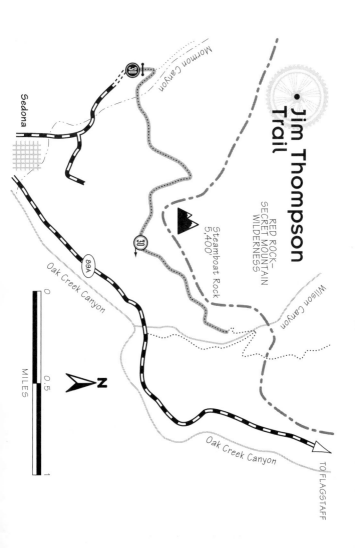

Jim Thompson
Trail

RED ROCK–
SECRET MOUNTAIN
WILDERNESS

Mormon Canyon

Sedona

Steamboat Rock
5,400'

Wilson Canyon

Oak Creek Canyon

89A

N

0   0.5   1
MILES

Oak Creek Canyon

TO FLAGSTAFF

113

Land status: Coconino National Forest.

Maps: USGS Wilson Mountain, Munds Park.

Access: From the junction of Arizona Highway 89A and AZ 179 in Sedona, drive north on AZ 89A about 0.4 mile, then turn left onto Jordan Road. In another 0.8 mile, turn left on Park Ridge Road, and continue to the trailhead at a locked gate (the last 0.2 mile is dirt).

The Ride

0.0   Ride around the gate and uphill on the wide Brins Mesa Trail.

0.1   Turn right at a cairn onto narrower singletrack, the Jim Thompson Trail. The first section of this trail is somewhat sandy and rocky as it descends slightly, then turns sharply left and starts to climb.

0.5   Pedal through a gate as the grade moderates.

0.7   Pedal east as the trail contours along the base of red rock cliffs.

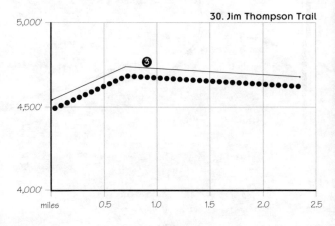

1.5   Stay left on the main trail.

2.3   The main trail goes left and drops into a canyon; stay right and ride a short, level loop that takes you to a great viewpoint and the turn-around point. (Though the trail continues to AZ 89A, which can be used to return to Sedona, I don't recommend this route because of heavy traffic on the narrow highway.)

Red Rock Loop

Location: Southwest of Sedona, near Oak Creek.

Distance: 10.1-mile loop.

Time: 2 hours.

Tread: 7.5 miles on paved road, 1.3 miles on maintained dirt road, 1.3 miles on singletrack.

Aerobic level: Moderate.

Technical difficulty: 1 on pavement, 2 on dirt road and singletrack.

Hazards: Watch for heavy tourist traffic on the paved road and a few rocky, rutted sections on the dirt road.

Highlights: This is a spectacular ride to historic Red Rock Crossing on Oak Creek.

Land status: Coconino National Forest, private.

Maps: USGS Sedona; Coconino National Forest.

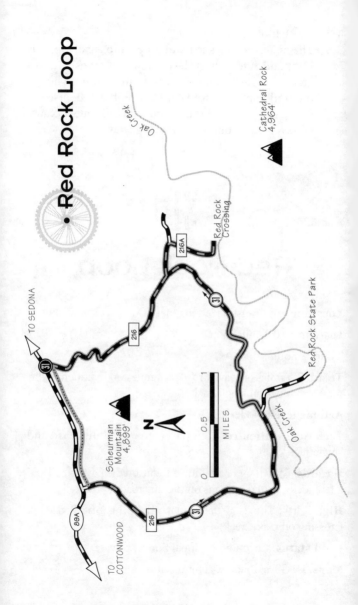

Red Rock Loop

TO SEDONA

89A

TO COTTONWOOD

216

216

Scheurman Mountain
4,899'

216A

Red Rock
Crossing

Cathedral Rock
4,964'

Oak Creek

Red Rock State Park

Oak Creek

N

MILES

0   0.5   1

Access: From the junction of Arizona Highway 89A and AZ 179 (the Y) in Sedona, drive west on AZ 89A through west Sedona. Turn left on the Upper Red Rock Loop Road at the signal, and park.

The Ride

0.0   Start by riding Red Rock Loop Trail, paralleling AZ 89A.

1.3   Turn left on Lower Red Rock Loop Road (Forest Road 216). This paved road is marked as a bicycle route. A gradual descent takes you into the broad valley west of Scheurman Mountain, and then around the southern tip of the mountain. Oak Creek is visible below to the south.

4.3   At the junction with the road to Red Rock State Park, continue straight ahead onto the dirt road. This section wanders in and out of gullies and over small hills; it can be rocky and rutted if not recently maintained.

5.6   Roll onto smooth pavement.

6.6   Turn right at the sign for Red Rock Crossing (FR 216A).

6.9   Go right again where signed for Red Rock Crossing.

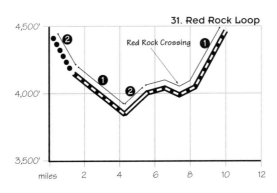

7.4 Red Rock Crossing, a popular creekside recreation area and one of the most photographed places in Arizona. Cathedral Rock is reflected in the waters of Oak Creek just above the old crossing. The ford washed out in a flood, and there's no longer a way to cross the creek. Ride back the way you came to rejoin the loop.

8.3 Bear right, joining the Upper Red Rock Loop Road (FR 216), which climbs steadily around the east side of Scheurman Mountain. This section has a wide shoulder, giving more room for bikes.

10.1 End of the ride at AZ 89A.

Schnebly Hill

Location: Just east of Sedona.

Distance: 12.8 miles out and back.

Time: 3 hours.

Tread: 11.8 miles on infrequently maintained dirt road, 1 mile on paved road.

Aerobic level: Moderate.

Technical difficulty: 1 on pavement, 2+ on dirt road.

Hazards: Watch for heavy traffic in the summer. The road can be rocky and full of potholes.

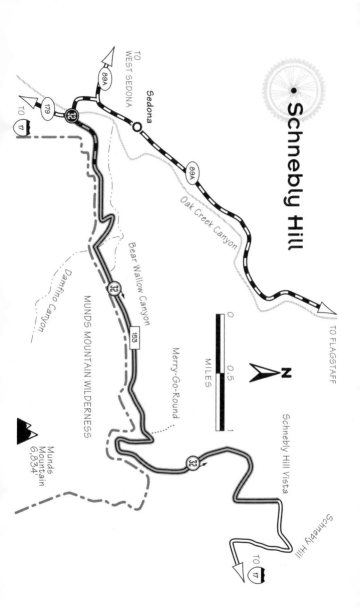

Schnebly Hill

TO WEST SEDONA

89A

179

TO 17

Sedona

89A

Oak Creek Canyon

TO FLAGSTAFF

Bear Wallow Canyon

Damfino Canyon

MUNDS MOUNTAIN WILDERNESS

153

Merry-Go-Round

N

MILES
0   0.5   1

Schnebly Hill Vista

Munds
Mountain
6,854

Schnebly Hill

TO 17

Highlights: Scenic ride through red rock formations and interesting geology to the Mogollon Rim, and a viewpoint overlooking Sedona and lower Oak Creek Canyon.

Land status: Coconino National Forest, private.

Maps: USGS Sedona, Munds Mountain, Munds Park; Coconino National Forest.

Access: From the junction of Arizona Highway 89A and AZ 179 (the Y) in Sedona, drive south on AZ 179 for 0.4 mile. Cross Oak Creek Bridge, then turn left on the Schnebly Hill Road (Forest Road 153) and park.

The Ride

0.0 Follow paved Schnebly Hill Road as it climbs through a residential area.

0.5 End of pavement. The dirt road (FR 153) is maintained, but its condition varies. You'll probably be picking your way around a rocky surface much of the way. The road generally follows the south side of Bear Wallow Canyon, dipping in and out of dry washes, and climbs gradually at first. Near the head of the canyon, it starts to climb more steeply as it switchbacks under the imposing cliffs of Munds Mountain. (The area south of the road is in the Munds Mountain Wilderness, and is closed to bikes.)

4.1 A singletrack branches left to Merry-Go-Round, a circular red rock formation that is a popular slickrock play area. Maybe you'll want to get the climb over first and play on the way down?

5.2 Ride through a pass and around a corner above Munds Canyon. Notice that the road surface is no longer red, but a dark reddish brown. Layers of basalt lava flows

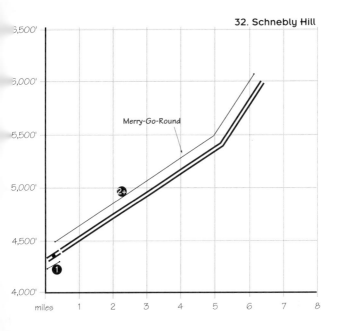

cover the rim above you—the last part of the climb is through these layers of volcanic rock. The road rounds the head of Munds Canyon and finishes the climb to the Mogollon Rim.

6.4 Schnebly Hill Vista, and the turn-around point. You're looking into lower Oak Creek Canyon. On the far side is Wilson Mountain, named for an early settler who was mauled by a grizzly bear. Grizzlies are extinct in Arizona, but black bears are still found in more remote areas.

33

Chapel Rocks Loop

Location: 3.5 miles south of Sedona.

Distance: 6.3-mile loop.

Time: 2 hours.

Tread: 1.7 miles on paved roads, 4.6 miles on singletrack.

Aerobic level: Moderate.

Technical difficulty: 1 on paved roads, 3+ on singletrack.

Hazards: Watch for a few steep, rocky sections, and for hikers, horses, and other cyclists.

Highlights: Spectacular loop ride around one of Sedona's famous rock formations, featuring smooth, fast singletrack and some slickrock play areas.

Land status: Coconino National Forest, private.

Maps: USGS Sedona, Munds Mountain.

Access: From the junction of Arizona Highway 89A and AZ 179 in Sedona, go south 3.5 miles on AZ 179, and park at the North Bell Rock Pathway Trailhead.

The Ride

0.0   From the parking area, start on the broad Bell Rock Pathway, then immediately hang a left on the narrower singletrack and head north, climbing gradually.

Chapel Rocks Loop

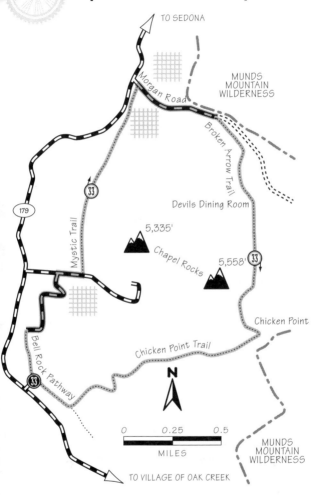

TO SEDONA

MUNDS MOUNTAIN WILDERNESS

Morgan Road

Broken Arrow Trail

179

33

Mystic Trail

Devils Dining Room

5,335'

Chapel Rocks

5,558'

33

Chicken Point

Chicken Point Trail

Bell Rock Pathway

33

N

0   0.25   0.5
MILES

MUNDS MOUNTAIN WILDERNESS

TO VILLAGE OF OAK CREEK

0.1 Bear to the left on singletrack marked with rock cairns in wire cages.

0.3 Pedal right on Indian Cliffs Road.

0.6 Go left on Badger Drive.

0.9 Now go right on Susan Way, then left on Geneva Drive then right on Chapel Road.

1.2 Turn left on Mystic Trail, a singletrack opposite Antelope Drive.

2.1 Roll onto Pine Knolls Drive.

2.2 Bear left on Pine Drive.

2.3 Go right on singletrack just before reaching AZ 89A.

2.5 Ride right on Morgan Road.

3.1 At the parking area where the jeep trail starts, turn right onto Broken Arrow Trail, a singletrack marked with cairns. This trail stays above the jeep trail and climbs along the base of the rocks through some slickrock areas. Watch for sudden, sharp descents.

3.7 Ride past a natural sink hole—the Devil's Dining Room.

4.0 Turn right on the Chicken Point Trail. You can go left to Submarine Rock, a slickrock play area, which adds 0.8 mile to the ride.

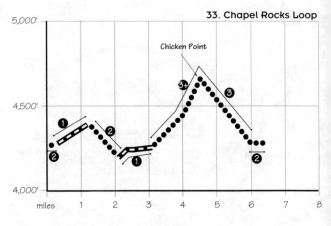

124

4.1 Stay right at a jeep trail.
4.5 Cross Chicken Point (actually, a pass), left, and descend Little Horse Trail along the east side of the ravine north of the pass. This singletrack is marked with cairns. Watch for steep, rocky descents.
5.6 Bear left, down into a gully.
5.9 Bear right, out of the gully.
6.0 Go right on Bell Rock Pathway, which is broad singletrack.
6.3 Hang a left into the trailhead to complete the loop.

Courthouse Butte

Location: About 6 miles south of Sedona near the Village of Oak Creek.

Distance: 2.8-mile loop.

Time: 30 minutes.

Tread: 2.8 miles on singletrack.

Aerobic level: Easy.

Technical difficulty: 2+.

Hazards: Watch for hikers and horses on this popular trail. Stay out of Munds Mountain Wilderness, which borders this ride on the north. Remain on the route and respect private property.

Highlights: Scenic, easy loop along the bases of Bell Rock and Courthouse Butte.

• Courthouse Butte

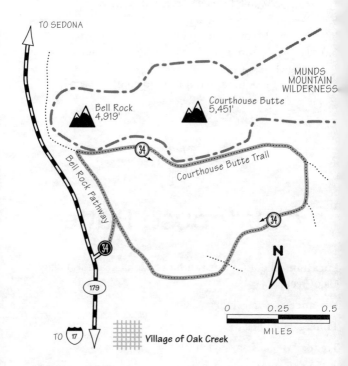

TO SEDONA

MUNDS
MOUNTAIN
WILDERNESS

Bell Rock
4,919'

Courthouse Butte
5,451'

(34)

Courthouse Butte Trail

Bell Rock Pathway

(34)

(34)

N

(34)

(179)

0   0.25   0.5
MILES

TO (17)

Village of Oak Creek

126

Land status: Coconino National Forest.

Maps: USGS Sedona, Munds Mountain.

Access: From the junction of Arizona Highway 89A and AZ 179 in Sedona, go south about 6 miles on AZ 179, and park at the South Bell Rock Pathway trailhead, which is just north of the Village of Oak Creek on the east side of the highway.

The Ride

0.0   Pedal up the broad, smooth surface of the Bell Rock Pathway toward Bell Rock.

0.6   Hang a right onto Courthouse Butte Trail, which is narrow singletrack. Stay on the main trail, contouring east along the base of towering Courthouse Butte.

1.5   Descend into a slickrock wash, then turn right, downhill.

1.8   Stay right at a fork.

2.0   Bear right on the main trail.

2.3   A minor trail crosses; go straight.

2.4   Pedal right at a fence. The parking area is visible to the west.

2.7   Stay left at a fork.

2.8   Go left onto the Bell Rock Pathway to the trailhead.

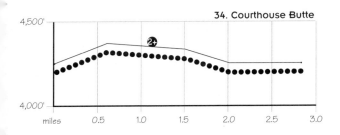

Hot Loop

Location: About 7 miles south of Sedona, in Woods Canyon.

Distance: 8.1-mile loop.

Time: 2 hours.

Tread: 3.1 miles on singletrack, 1.2 miles on doubletrack, 3.8 miles on paved roads.

Aerobic level: Moderate.

Technical difficulty: 3+ on singletrack, 2 on doubletrack, 1 on paved roads.

Hazards: Some rocky sections. Watch for hikers and horses.

Highlights: This is an enjoyable loop along the edge of the Munds Mountain Wilderness with some fine, smooth singletrack.

Land status: Coconino National Forest.

Maps: USGS Munds Mountain, Sedona; Coconino National Forest.

Access: From the junction of Arizona Highway 89A and AZ 179 (the Y) in Sedona, drive about 7 miles south on AZ 179 to the Village of Oak Creek. Turn left at the traffic light onto Jacks Canyon Road and go 0.9 mile. Turn right to remain on Jacks Canyon Road. After another 1.1 miles, turn right at the sign for Hot Loop Trail, and drive 0.3 mile to the parking area.

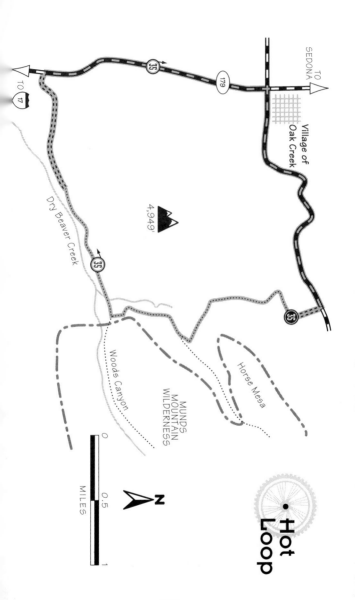

TO
SEDONA

Village of
Oak Creek

179

35

35

TO 17

Dry Beaver Creek

35

4,949'

35

Woods Canyon

MUNDS
MOUNTAIN
WILDERNESS

Horse Mesa

MILES

0   0.5   1

N

• Hot
Loop

The Ride

0.0 Pedal up the singletrack as it climbs along the pinyon-juniper covered slopes of Horse Mesa. There are a few rocky and steep sections.

0.8 Cross over a pass, through a wire gate, and start the descent into Woods Canyon. Watch for rocky sections.

1.3 Go right, downhill, at an unsigned junction. (The left fork enters the Munds Mountain Wilderness, which is closed to bikes.)

2.0 Turn right again and cruise the singletrack down Woods Canyon. (The left fork also enters the Munds Mountain Wilderness.)

3.1 Pass a Munds Mountain Wilderness sign, and follow the doubletrack west as it climbs slightly and leaves the

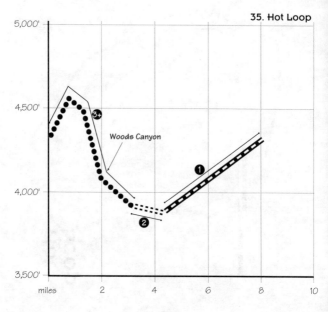

35. Hot Loop

canyon bottom. (The actual wilderness boundary is just east of the trail over Horse Mesa, and all of this ride is outside the wilderness.)

4.3   Pedal right (north) on AZ 179, which has a broad shoulder.

5.8   Go right at the traffic light onto Jacks Canyon Road.

7.8   Turn right one more time at the Hot Loop Trailhead sign.

8.1   Trailhead and your vehicle.

Appendix A
Information Sources

Flagstaff Planning Division
211 West Aspen
Flagstaff, AZ 86001
(520) 779-7632

Sedona Parks and Recreation
525 Posse Grounds Road
Sedona, AZ 86336
(520) 282-7098

Coconino National Forest
Beaver Creek Ranger District
H.C. 64, Box 240
Rimrock, AZ 86335
(520) 567-4501

Coconino National Forest
Mormon Lake Ranger District
4825 South Lake Mary Road
Flagstaff, AZ 86001
(520) 774-1147

Coconino National Forest
Peaks Ranger District
5075 North Highway 89
Flagstaff, AZ 86004
(520) 526-0866

Coconino National Forest
Sedona Ranger District
P.O. Box 300
Sedona, AZ 86336-0300
(520) 282-4119

Coconino National Forest
Supervisor's Office
2323 East Greenlaw Lane
Flagstaff, AZ 86001
(520) 527-3600

Kaibab National Forest
Chalender/Williams Ranger District
Route 1 Box 142
501 West Route 66
Williams, AZ 86046
(520) 635-2633

Kaibab National Forest
Supervisor's Office
800 South 6th Street
Williams, AZ 86046
(520) 635-8200

Kaibab National Forest
Tusayan Ranger District
P.O. Box 3088
Tusayan, AZ 86023
(520) 638-2443

Kaibab National Forest
Williams and Forest Service
Visitor Center
200 West Railroad Avenue
Williams, AZ 86046
(520) 635-4061

Arizona Game and Fish Department
3500 South Lake Mary Road
Flagstaff, AZ 86001
(520) 774-5045

Arizona State Land Department
3650 Lake Mary Road
Flagstaff, AZ 86001
(520) 774-1425

U.S. Geological Survey
Map Distribution Branch
P.O. Box 25286
Denver Federal Center
Denver, CO 80225

Appendix B
Bike Shops

Absolute Bikes
18 North San Francisco Street
Flagstaff, AZ 86001
(520) 779-5969

Cosmic Cycles
113 South San Francisco Street
Flagstaff, AZ 86001
(520) 779-1092

Flagstaff Bicycle and Fitness
2404 East Route 66
Flagstaff, AZ 86001
(520) 526-2780

Loose Spoke
1529 South Milton Road
Flagstaff, AZ 86001
(520) 774-7428

Mountain Sports
1800 South Milton Road
Flagstaff, AZ 86001
(800) 286-5156
(520) 779-5156

Single Track Bikes
12 North Beaver Street
Flagstaff, AZ 86001
(520) 773-1862

Sedona Bike and Bean Shoppe
376 Jordon Road
Sedona, AZ 86336
(520) 282-3515

Mountain Bike Heaven
1695 West Highway 89A
Sedona, AZ 86336
(520) 282-1312

A Short Index of Rides

Glossary

ATB: All-terrain bicycle; a.k.a. mountain bike, sprocket rocket, fat tire flyer.

ATV: All-terrain vehicle; in this book ATV refers to motorbikes and three- or four-wheelers designed for off-road use.

Bail: Getting off the bike, usually in a hurry, and whether or not you mean to. Often a last resort.

Bunny hop: Leaping up, while riding, and lifting both wheels off the ground to jump over an obstacle (or for sheer joy).

Butt ruff: A rocky trail that pounds the rider through the saddle, especially on descent. Will this term become obsolete with the spread of fully suspended bikes?

Cairn: A pile of stones used to mark a trail.

Clean: To ride without touching a foot (or other body part) to the ground; to ride a tough section successfully.

Clipless pedal: A type of pedal with a binding that accepts a matching cleat on the sole of a bike shoe. The cleat locks to the pedal for more control and efficient pedaling, and is easily unlatched for safe landings (in theory).

Contour: A line on a topographic map showing a continuous elevation level over uneven ground. Also a verb indicating a fairly easy or moderate grade: "The trail contours around the west flank of the mountain before the final grunt to the top."

Dab: To put a foot or a hand down (or to hold onto or lean on a tree or other support) while riding. If you have to dab, then you haven't ridden that piece of trail clean.

Downfall: Trees that have fallen across the track (also deadfall).

Doubletrack: A trail, jeep road, ATV route, or other track with two distinct ribbons of tread, typically with grass growing in between. No matter which side you choose, the other rut always looks smoother.

Endo: Lifting the rear wheel off the ground and riding (or abruptly not riding) on the front wheel only. Also known, at various degrees of control and finality, as a nose wheelie, "going over the handlebars," and a face plant.

Fall line: The angle and direction of a slope; the line you follow when gravity is in control and you aren't.

Graded: When a gravel road is scraped smooth to level out the washboards and potholes, it has been graded. In this book, a road is listed as graded only if it is regularly maintained. Even these roads are not always graded every year.

Granny gear: The lowest combination of gears for climbing. Shift down to the innermost and smallest of the chainrings on the bottom bracket spindle (where the pedals and crank arms attach to the bike's frame) and up to the biggest cog on the rear hub to find your granny gear.

Hammer: To ride hard; derived from how it feels afterward: "I'm hammered."

Hammerhead: Someone who actually enjoys feeling hammered. A Type A rider who goes hard and fast all the time.

Kelly hump: An abrupt mound of dirt across the road or trail. These are common on old logging roads and skidder tracks, placed there to block vehicle access. At high speeds, they become launching pads that transform bikes into satellites and riders into astronauts.

Line: The route (or trajectory) between or over obstacles or through turns. Tread or trail refers to the ground you're riding on; the line is the path you choose within the tread (and exists mostly in the eye of the beholder).

Off-the-seat: Moving your butt behind the bike seat and over the rear tire; used for control on extremely steep descents. This position increases braking power, helps prevent endos, and reduces skidding.

Portage: To carry the bike, usually up a steep hill, across unrideable obstacles, or through a stream.

Quads: Thigh muscles (short for quadriceps); or maps in the USGS topographic series (short for quadrangles). The right quads (of either kind) can prevent or get you out of trouble in the backcountry.

Ratcheting: Also known as backpedaling; pedaling backwards to avoid bashing feet or pedals on rocks or other obstacles.

Sidehill: Where the trail crosses a slope's fall line. If the **tread** is narrow, keep your uphill pedal up to avoid hitting the ground. If the tread has a sideways slant, you may have to use body English to keep the bike vertical and avoid side-slipping.

Singletrack: A trail, game run, or other track with only one ribbon of tread. Singletrack is pure fun.

Spur: A side road or trail that splits off from the main route.

Surf: Riding through loose gravel or sand, when the wheels slalom from side to side. Also heavy surf: frequent and difficult obstacles.

Suspension: A bike with front suspension has a shock-absorbing fork or stem. Rear suspension absorbs shock between the rear wheel and frame. A bike with both is said to be fully suspended.

Switchbacks: When a trail goes up a steep slope, it zig zags or switchbacks across the **fall line** to ease the gradient of the climb. Well-designed switchbacks make a turn with at least an eight-foot radius and remain fairly level within the turn itself. These are rare, however, and cyclists often struggle through sharply angled, sloping switchbacks.

Tank: A small, seasonal pond with an earthen dam built by ranchers as a water source for cattle.

Track stand: Balancing on a bike in one place, without rolling forward appreciably. Cock the front wheel to one side and bring that pedal up to the 1 or 2 o'clock position. Now control your side-to-side balance by applying pressure on the pedals and brakes and changing the angle of the front wheel, as needed. It takes practice but really comes in handy at stoplights, on **switchbacks**, and when trying to free a foot before falling. (See **clipless pedal**.)

Tread: The riding surface, particularly regarding singletrack.

Water bar: A log, rock, conveyor belting, ditch, or other barrier placed in the **tread** to divert water off the trail and prevent erosion. Peeled logs can be slippery and cause bad falls, especially when they angle sharply across the trail.

About the Author

Bruce Grubbs is an avid hiker, mountain biker, and cross-country skier who has been exploring the American desert for over 30 years. An outdoor writer and photographer, he has written eight other FalconGuides. He lives in Flagstaff, Arizona.